Here is a spooky book to
keep you on your toes on
those cool spring nights...

E xx

Canst thou draw out leviathan with an hook?

About the author

Giles Goodland was born in Taunton in 1964, studied at Lampeter and U.C. Santa Cruz, and at Oxford wrote a doctoral thesis on British modernism in 1940s film and poetry. His own poetry has been published widely in the past decade, has won several competitions, and earned him a major Eric Gregory Award in 1994 and a Hawthornden fellowship in 1998. He has published three pamphlets as well as a previous book-length poem, *Littoral* (1996), and has also had two plays performed. Giles Goodland lives in London, and works on a dictionary.

By the same author

A SPY IN
THE HOUSE
OF YEARS

GILES GOODLAND

LEVIATHAN

First published in Great Britain in 2001 by
Leviathan
Ivory's Farm
Burnt House Lane
Cowfold
Horsham RH13 8DQ

© Giles Goodland, 2001

Giles Goodland is hereby identified as the author of this work
in accordance with the Copyright, Designs and Patents Act 1988

A CIP record for this book is available from the British Library

ISBN   1-903563-08-9 (cased)
1-903563-09-7 (paperback)

Editorial Director
Michael Hulse

Editorial Advisers
David Hartnett, John Kinsella, Anne Michaels, Vincent O'Sullivan

Design
Claire Brodmann

Typesetting
Birgit Beyer

Printing and Binding
T.J. International Ltd., Padstow, Cornwall PL28 8RW

Contents

Acknowledgements

Versions of these poems have appeared in *Edinburgh Review, Fire, Illuminations, Journal of Contemporary Anglo-Scandinavian Poetry, Prop* and *Southfields*.

A SPY IN THE HOUSE
OF YEARS

1900

There is no true poet who has not again and again been mastered by that strange feeling of helplessness in the hands of

the automotive actions of vegetative life. — Under this head we have: (a) those of the respiratory neuro-mechanism; (b) those of the

loss of the power of naming objects or of recognizing names

"Who was it?" said he. At once the spirit indicated a desire to use the alphabet

the connection was made, and I called up one part of the globe after another, and looked upon its life, and realized that by grace of this marvelous instrument I

mobbed two preachers, tarred and feathered them, and rode them on a rail because they preached the doctrine of

big, manly-looking, self-reliant Dick taking his position to strike

surrounded by a "pearl" or "loop" occasionally made more beautiful and complicated by

the trim garden of the nineteenth-century hotel slowly made the scene of gradually growing

tears in my eyes somehow gave me a kind of poetic pleasure

seemed to grieve the kind-hearted Munchkins for they immediately took out their handkerchiefs and began to

act without my conscious volition. Now and then I tell them to keep off the grass

world of the occult shines through the commonplace earth-bound reality. These residual phenomena afford a glimpse of the

mythopoetical effect, which for us comes only with time, takes place at once, and swells to heroic proportions.

1901

The public look upon the old lady as a kind of fetish or idol, and nobody will dare print a word not to her glorification

or, if not possible, being contrite and invoking the name of "Jesus", at least (if not able otherwise) in her heart, and accepting death in a patient spirit from the hand of God

a series of pictures of the day's doings passed before her imagination like the roll of a Kinetoscope

"time-sense" apparatus, consisting of Baltzar kymograph, time-disc, set of contacts, and

the adventitial lymphatic sheath

of a woman who has died in child-bed. She haunts lonely roads, her feet are turned backwards on the ankles, and she leads men to

imagine a white dress made with a fitted bodice fastened invisibly down the front

the girth of its body was some fourscore feet, its length perhaps two hundred

she carried plenty of Brown Hair that she Built Up by putting Rats under

all human and personal ties, and you endeavour, in vain, to replace them by the impersonal activity of

gigantic incubators vomiting forth at pipping-time

to regulate, to maintain, and at the same time to refrigerate the innate heat of the heart

he implored the engine driver to hack off his foot, promising to make him a rich man

blood ebbs away from the brain because it is time for the brain to rest.

1902

The phonograph records of a fellow's character are lined in his face

on a flattened disc rotating horizontally, diminishing from the
circumference to the centre

the stories told of these men are translated from contemporary records,
and are curiously interesting as revealing the inner life

obtained by these solemn follies. They comprise the transposition of
letters in a given word

in addition to the rotatory or revolutionary movements of the foetus
there are others of a rhythmical kind of which tracings can be made by
means of a graphic apparatus

I filled three sheets of paper with it; then I got a carbon and
manifolded it

in a little railway station on the Victorian side of the border. A woman
of the party became suddenly unwell and brought a little stranger into
the world

a short, thickset man with full beard got out and entered the tavern,
registered, and was assigned to the corner room over the office

had a low "difference-threshold" — his mind easily steps over it into
the consciousness of the differences in question

sung a comic song and was in the middle of a breakdown when he
caught the eye of the old man fixed on him and a lugubrious voice said

that guy that doped me, he wa'nt satisfied with my good thirty-dollar
wad

full of charm and freshness and simplicity, will appeal to all who like
sometimes in quiet moments to

empty lakes, drain peat-mosses, embank rivers, grub up forests, turn
grass into arable land and arable again into grass, and, last

how the first night they slept without blinds, with the moon looking in
on the pale child who soon grew.

1903

If full use is made of the means by which the world of phenomena offers to theory

what looks like a retouch above the man's left shoulder turns out on closer inspection to be

this delightful facility, with such a woman, of arriving at a new tone; he thought, as he lay on his back, of all the tones she might make possible

where the Harmony Society established

the combined use of a distinctly Swedish apparatus called the plinth, and a chest machine

the pinnacle of my happiness, from which I was in a little while dashed to earth

a "doped" cigar was given to her in a pool and billiard room, and

her thoughts presented themselves in visual forms attended by an hallucinatory

dove-shaped pyx of precious metal, suspended over an altar by a chain from the roof

served with half a dozen tablespoonfuls of consommé, or petite marmite, or

a complex liquid heavily charged with dead organic matter, which, though perhaps more offensive than injurious when fresh, rapidly changes its nature

by presenting the history of England to them in a fresh and attractive way by means of typical lives of men and women, drawn from original sources

numerically, the words of Latin and Greek derivation preponderate, but this is somewhat deceptive, because a large proportion coming under this head have

radiants which give out N-rays communicating a similar variety of radio-activity.

1904

In fiction, whether it is historic, society, or the work of literary rough-housers

our lives are a congeries of solipsisms, out of which in strict logic only a God could compose a universe even of discourse

a perforated round symbol of cerulean tint is used in the worship of heaven, an octagonal symbol of yellow jade for

the various alphabet-using forms of amateur mediumship, such as table-tipping, the "Ouija-board", and certain other devices

fitted with an equilibrium valve, rendering the supply automatic and constant

spumed in my diary rather than my life

my inmost thoughts were being Röntgened

no mouthpiece is mine. I've got to be sprung on paper or go to the jungle

with our improved burner. Agents coming our way. Enormous demand. Sells at sight

sheds water out of the holes it looks with, and wipes it away with the backs of its paws

'tis nothing when you are used to it, as the eels said when they were being skinned alive

with this instrument the bone may be broken above the condyles at the desired point

used, following Prof. Seuss, as the equivalent of "massive unstratified limestones and dolomites", strikingly contrasted sediments

yet the early investigators extrapolated from this linearity all across the mysteries of set, yield-point, and stricture, up to rupture.

1905

Through the soft music of the cultured voices around her there crept an ominous hiss as the little green head parted the perfumed lace

and, as the trunk opened, I shrank back. It was filled with a mass of mossy white-and-green mould from which cockroaches darted in all

greens — eau de nil, vert-doré, aquamarine, and emerald

for nearly two years, when the little fairy-man with the green suit again drew near the road where

his overcoat was beginning to wear a greenish shade and look threadbare. When his toilet was complete he looked at

the green time-stained panes of the windows looking upon each other with the cowardly glances of

painful march. Assembled on the green, all was ready, when Major Pitcairn, remembering the little woman who

saw through the mist a pair of keen, malicious eyes, which appeared to her excited brain to have a supernatural green light

noticed some tall lilies, which grew on both sides of the way, with dazzlingly white flowers, set off by the universal green. It was now dark enough to see that

I always had big green eyes." "I love your queer eyes. They always look as if they

may contain brain-substance (*encephalocele*) or brain-substance and fluid (*encephalomeningocele*)

They both laughed, and he knelt by the table to light the lamp under the kettle, while she measured out the tea into a little tea-pot of green gauze

to justify the alarmists who speak of the beverage as "the green peril"

towards the end of the twentieth century. The meadows were no longer green.

1906

I read it eagerly and re-read it and went on re-re-reading

of the approach of a body of Pinkerton detectives

they discovered Chinamen on every floor in various stages of ecstacy, besides coming on a bunch of Celestials in the act of hitting the pipe

rounding Tattenham Corner, Troutbeck resumed the lead, closely pursued by Picton, His Eminence, and Spearmint, with Malua and Beppo side by side, well clear of

the rector and rectress, and their two delicate-looking, perfectly-dressed daughters

overtaken by a desperate fit of sobbing

who had been in "the profession" as a Fat Girl, had come down in the world

burnt a few punk sticks in the joss house to

the more or less sexual pleasure sometimes experienced in the sight of copulating animals

which suggests that conation attaches to the visual reaction by association through memory with

any set of signs which are so connected that a complex of two of them must be Determinants of one Sign which is a quasi-mind

what else are we to make of a boy who missed an engagement with a girl because he was absorbed in Hegel's philosophy when he ought to have

travelled around the free border of the bone, through the muco-periosteum on the outer side, and then point as a gumboil

which led the poet into some bitter literary disputes and were discussed in Europe for a hundred years.

1907

Here again, the implication of the thinking situation is of some "correspondence" between two sets of distinguished relations; the probem of the

clink of chips. For it was the grave-yard gamblers shift

we sometimes hear vague thinkers speak as if during the evolution of organic life animal instinct

will extend from the North Sea to Persia, including the Western half of Russia, all because it has been the first to develop aerial navigation, and to lead the

great twanging of strings that was going on in reply to Will's insistent "a-a-a" on the piano, and low breathing of flute and piccolo

then the silent Indian would hack off his head with a flint and pickle it for

this selfish onesidedness of the tone of feeling exists in many born criminals, also in the pseudo-querulants, where

every variation from normal breathing, due to emotional suggestion, is marked by the machine. Each expiration writes its own history

writes well because when he writes his mind is as nearly normal as possible

they'd put him in a narrow grave and pour quicklime on his

receptacle for human excreta, together with the structure comprising such receptacle and the fittings and apparatus connected therewith

Transformation Fire, red and green, suitable for indoor use

employees assisted many of the frightened girls to cross from the blazing building to the Gramophone recording rooms

and then the ambulance will take them to the hospital where the grinning skulls of their predecessors are stored.

1908

Where as the defendant himself expresses a belief that his brain is dusty and also expresses a desire to "do a bit" in the booby hatch, we, the honourable members of the bug commission

tabulated the narcotics according to the smallest molecular concentration which produced definite physiological effect

yet the tremors of tongue and lip are not met with

each girl sits in front of a relay rack, fitted with a bewildering number of small holes

"I'd like to have the job which goes with that blonde," and I pointed to a pippin who was pounding the

MARX PIANO HARP. This instrument is picked with the right hand, while the hammers are manipulated with the left hand

when the last shadow of separateness melts back into a complete néant of silence, of not hearing, not knowing — being left to feel that I

shall I say plagiarised Time's methods

with every prospect of a good fight. The Utman Khel, 3,000 in number, were strongly placed on our line of advance

among them is the verb *make*, the article on which fills eleven pages, and would have been much longer if every subtle variety of meaning had been explained and illustrated

with all his specialist knowledge he could not place Methuselahism among the variations of Protestantism. The soldier replied that it was his religion "to live as long as he could

escape death narrowly in about 5 different ways — such as drowning, smashing into smithereens, brain fever, "exposure" (!) etc etc

and by then I shall be old and ugly, and probably deaf, but I hope not dumb, and all the sap will have run out of my

vignetting or arabesquing fringe and atmosphere of exaggeration and fantasy.

1909

The argument of this chapter is that parenthood must be forbidden to the dipsomaniac, the chronic inebriate or

a friend of mine who has a remarkable faculty of automatic writing sends me the following autoscript which she

set in a face whose expression was that innocence of a mind which knows and has put aside until

drunk, eh? Spifflicated, pie-eyed, loaded, sloshed

the consumptives who regularly frequent these places expectorate millions of living and active bacilli; and these are

the terrible fluidity of self-revelation

Dick may have been on the queer all right, but he was smooth enough

to just say to this wonderful sub-mind when you are going to sleep, "Soul, I desire to have now, while my conscious mind is in abeyance

separation of the races in trains, street-carts, etc., to save the white people from occasional contact with drunken, ill-smelling negroes

less and less capable of performing certain actions. He could not walk and could not pronounce perfectly, owing to these little processes becoming contracted, and ultimately

Atlee, who was the librarian in charge of the Archives, was shocked at this and insisted that he should restore the page and write an acknowledgement of its having been torn out

I was sorry to observe a large number of undergraduates present, all mingling freely with the roughs and shop-girls

but we refused to take it, because we thought that the oil was made from the bones of the dead men we had seen

should test the value of CLARKE'S BLOOD MIXTURE The World-famed Blood Purifier and Restorer. Refuse substitutes.

1910

It is probably true that the preadolescent girl can pursue her school work side by side with the boy

it must be pressed out with the blackhead instrument, if steaming and massage fail to remove it

it shows itself in the form of red pimples or papules, which may become pustular and

it consists essentially of an oscillating plunger pump worked by an eccentric on the crank-shaft, the oscillations of the pump-barrel being utilised to discharge

a new bright black shot with purple, the "ravens-wing" glaze of the collectors

it is probable that the fissure results from the tearing down of one of the anal valves

(the almost man) in his human delineation of the Darwinean theory

as a agnosticle stoker psalm-singin' 'imself up the Service under a pious captain

had fallen in love with her when she had first taken Marseilles captive with

honest, beef-bred blood boils in his swollen

ranks of prophets of Earth's dissolution — all nations banded together to work Evil

what I don't let him savvy is, whether I care a twopenny damn for him

black and scarred, and this crown of raw flesh was the size of

vain hands in the rosy mists of poets' experiences.

1911

Oneness and homogeneity could be evolved from such apparently relationless short-cut phrases as

an inscription (we will say) or an important textual variation: it is then misinterpreted to fit a pre-conceived theory; then

table IX shows the average rates of interest yielded by investments in bonds and by short-term loans for the successive phases of each business cycle since

I was ushered into the Poet's large dark oak sitting room with its huge log fires burning; I could hear the clash of knives and forks in the adjoining apartment which

claim to have heard unborn children breathe and cry

colloquial, facetious, slang, and vulgar expressions with freedom, merely attaching a cautionary label

smells are usually the first symptoms of such derangement, but not invariably

I once saw Chirgwin, the White-eyed Kaffir, "guyed" by some young gentlemen in a box at the London Pavilion. He let them amuse themselves for a time, then he pointed to the box and said

a deeper, more adult-like quack of two syllables, uttered in excitement in

the revival of an instinct that has been dormant for untold generations

spreading very thin layers of rubber on textiles for waterproofing or other purposes

sellers of canes, whips, and horns, and workers of small fortune-telling and gambling devices, were making

accounts of transitivity conducted in terms of "actor-action-patient"

something of the kind must be done or else writing becomes a mere debauch of the imagination.

1912

These "parasitic" foetuses are never born alone; they are the twin of a normal child

the heat causes the cylinder and the piston rings to expand until at last they become jammed irremovably

against the overmantel, obscured by a plush-bound photograph of Mr. Lloyd George

a goil would be a mutt to stay cocked up at home. An' yet a goil couldn't go chasin' around by her lonesome

stammered the lady, dropping the letter into her lap, and patting with agitated fingers her cap, her curls

the mist had thickened to a white, infinitesimal rain-dust

and the slightest moisture in the air was liable to draw them down into lank and unsightly plasters

she's the kippiest kid that ever lisped. Fed the angel on lobster and champagne last evening

whose symptoms were traced to repressions due to the sudden death of her fiancé

which ensues in the unconscious feelings of the physician through the influence of the patient

I felt a slight shudder under my hand and released my grip

I have faults, vices, beastliness but even with them I do believe you ought to marry me & be in love

shifted his position and came at the jury from another intellectual angle

I call to remembrance Oechalia's daughter, who, ere Love 'neath his tyrannous car-yoke had brought her, had been spouseless and free.

1913

Between what matters and what seems to matter, how should the world we know judge wisely?

the thinking, word-arranging, clarifying faculty must move and leap with the

dance halls and the tea tables, the queer wire-manufactured music

shining nickel-plated or aluminium utensils, including coffee percolators, toasters, chafing dishes, each with its long connecting cord and plug for attachment to

big red-and-white cheeks, plastic lips made for kissing and laughing; and her bare

worms were driven into the T by light and the chief motive for escape therefrom was

an eternal fundamental substance from which all phenomenal nature arises

basing his procedure on a knowledge of the dominance or recessiveness of each character the breeder may thus

diagnose the trouble as a neurosis, had it not been for the fact that the sexual anamnesis was so energetically denied by the patient

like the linty, raw-cold dust disturbed from the floor of a disused room

had been abruptly deserted once Reginald discovered that she used a certain cologne, which he decided

contrasts the "manifest content" which is the dream as directly related, with the "latent content", which is the group of thoughts reached by

confessing the truth even to her inmost soul, but the truth was there, and set her a-tremble with

words until the laws of heredity consent to unify the capacities of men.

1914

I do not hesitate to appropriate another's utterance when I can use it to good advantage, and therefore

the reflection and what it mirrors have equal force, and we ourselves seem hardly more than one of the things which we contemplate

a simple old-fashioned song with a note of futurism in its very lyric refrain

most wile 'bout mah Jelly-Roll

he saw the young man's breast heaving as he made an effort of words

logical so-called propositions shew logical properties of language and therefore of Universe, but say nothing

we, as physical machines, are built on a scale which is large compared with light waves and electrons, from which

a world of reals, each of which can only be perceived by one creature from one space

incline one way and three or four of my colleagues incline the other

by the wayside and at the entrance to valleys, stand demon-posts, rudely cut with grinning teeth and horrible faces

in proceeding to whatever the consequences may be and whatever measures may be forced upon us by the development of facts or action taken by others

mirrored on the placid pool; the fierce and terrible features of the ape beside those of the aristocratic

map bristling with wax-headed pins of great variety in size and colour. They represented

himself as a ludicrous figure, orating to vulgarians and idealizing his own clownish lusts, the pitiable fatuous fellow he had caught a glimpse of in the mirror.

1915

I have often picked up on the surface of the camp pieces of old root-eaten human bones

bits of brilliant stone, crystals and agates and onyx, and petrified wood as red as

the intelligence of his soil. The sovereign ghost

was in a violent state of excitement, and blew a police whistle

struggling for freedom under the oppression of things stored for reference in his capacious memory

withdrawing his senses, mind, and intellect from the outside, he turns the full concentrated current of will on

toad-spotted, raw-meat-coloured skin

secretion of tears, sighing, psychogalvanic phenomena, changes in the pulse

pride in the pursuance of the evanescent self down the printed page

the power of the body to convert latent into kinetic energy is

closed in the little nowhere of the brain

a sort of psychical decerebration

and with her blond wig properly tousled and her face turned always towards the rock wall, lest the camera should reveal the fact that

things that seemed disjointed are beginning to link themselves together, and the broken bones of history are rising from the battlefields.

1916

Here is no prose, here is not even English, but merely a flux of words

are played, stories are told, poetry is read, and lantern slides are shown;
its special aim is to deepen purity of thought among the girls

my thoughts just now lack grip and coherence and I feel that to
attempt to write should aid in altering this

some lover of an older day has carved in time-blurred lettering

I don't want my cranium shot away

a kind of thought which aims at providing a quasi-rational ground for
the indulgence of impulse

& go up on a mt. the first decent day I'm not painting — haven't any
paints — don't want them

to draw some picture in detail of the really marvellous movement
which since last July has covered England in new munitions factories
and added enormously to the

bubble of air blown into the centre of a mass of molten glass

individual emotions mirrored perfectly in a lucid supple periodic prose

with asphyxiating and lachrymatory shells

shattering and avalanching on the snow crust

when the incredible folly of the world must be tabloided into wisdom

never more shall I put on paper verse for the sake of a twisted conceit.

1917

Sirs: I am writing to find out if there is any way that you could find me a job. I would be very glad for you to do so and I will see that you wont loose nothing

the black and merciless things that are behind the great possessions

ghosts of children in gutters and on doorsteps proclaiming by their clay-coloured faces and underfed bodies the post-datement of the millenium

have freed political prisoners and burned police stations and police papers

the back-stairs politician foregathers with the cosmopolitan Financier and the cranky Pacifist

their composite paunchiness, beardedness, scragginess, impressed me unfavourably

a blotch of pallor stirs beneath the high square picture-dusk, the window of dark sky

all of us, sitting in darkness, saw a great light. You danced as dance the morning stars

with a play in verse that no manager would dream of; there were mistakes in grammar, in spelling of course, and worse. There were such phrases as

put your lamps over my shiners, run your hooks over me Astrakhan collar

as seen in idiots, cretins, and certain ethnic groups, due to a reversion to the

sea-voyage tale in which a hero, accompanied by a few companions, wanders from island to island, meets Otherworld wonders everywhere, and finally returns

thinking of a body X which *continues to exist* while the movement from A to B is occurring

I can't associate myself with the author, I seem to have quite outgrown him. I wonder if he really was myself.

1918

Yesterday morning at two o'clock peace was signed at Brest-Litovsk
between the Central Powers and the Ukrainian Rada

in my dream, I thought I held your hand and asked you to tell me what
your thoughts were. And you said

winds from sternward bore us out onward with bellying canvas, Circe's
this craft

this journey will come back vividly when I hear or think of an utterly
absurd song, which everyone sings, hums, whistles and shouts, "Good-
bye-ee

while in the purring greenery the crowd

and money both behave like loose quicksilver in a nest of cracks

sheckles, iron men, jack, cartwheels, kopex, mazuma, palm grease, evil
metal, jingles, liberty bait, armor plate, holy stones, joy berries

till my soul begins to burst with emotion or till something par trop
ridicule sets me roaring with laughter

some days he take his violin out of his box and make with his fingers
on the strings, like this, but never he

will set a train of impulse relays in the selector which act as
intermediaries to energise particular relays for the required

raspiness and blatancy which inevitably characterise horn machines

removal of his hat disclosed a Dutch-cut of yellow hair, blue eyes,
many little freckles, and an expression of

your ever trusted and uncompromising soul come forward again from
the unforgotten past

and in the happy no-time of his sleeping Death took him by the heart.

1919

Brooding music, faint and far-off, like the mood of the moonlight made audible

the phenomena of sleep walking and moon walking must be acknowledged almost entirely as

the skill which made the Lewis machine gun the wonderful weapon it turned out to be

eyes vacuum-cleaned of every speck of matter not germane to the functioning of pure, unmetamorphosed sight

Lenin stood there quite calmly, gripping the desk with both hands, his little eyes thoughtfully surveying the tumult beneath

might have doped out a corking yarn about how the Phantom made everybody believe that the explosion

functions as a schistose matrix in which the fragments of the more obdurate rocks float as isolated lenticles or

substitutes "meaning" for "copying" by an impossible use of "meaning" — an idea "standing for"

the faint and regular pulsation of her heart, firm and quick

exclusively composed of contents repressed from the conscious

to create a neutral strip or zone between their territory and Estonia, and would declare this

My Adventures in Picture Land

which may be conceived as a flat or homaloid locus in our present auxiliary five-fold continuum

largely in vain; the border-line is too vague and wavering to be adequately mapped; words and phrases constantly cross it.

1920

I may commend as a model to critics who desire to correct some of the poetical vagaries of the present age, the following

the great army of those employed in the liquor business has been demobilised

of time at a point in space. The aggregate of all the point-events is called the world

a clever and in its way convincing argument, but unhappily, if it is accepted, it destroys the whole British scheme

the heat of the day and the horror of this conversation were reducing his weight at the rate of ounces a minute

the only thing I understood was the "Prof's" last dozen or so words to the effect that some sort of experiment would be tried on a dog and we would conclude in prayer

the subject, with abdominal pneumographs attached, was lying on his back, and breathed as deeply as possible in time with a metronome

the world appears to it as a series of complicated moving surfaces

ascribed to the influence of the Irish, Indian seditionist and German groups, and all those factions whose world activities are hindered by the machinery of law and order maintained by

Professor W—, accustomed to take a daily walk with another old professor, when they discussed matters beyond the comprehension of ordinary mortals

huge crowds of workmen throughout Europe, these masses will gladly shed the blood of those of whom, in their ignorance, they have

tested by examining the quotations presented; this reveals, first, that many of them are but partial statements and

the doctor used the quotations to emphasize his own views, not because a message from my subliminal self had found

souls merely desired sufferings as the unavoidable price of an other-worldly reward.

1921

A message from the radio-room, sir

she felt strange and inevitable, as if she were centred upon the pivot of all existence, there was no further reality

she had yards upon yards of point de Venise in her top bureau-drawer

her force of character, emerging at length in all its plenitude, imposed itself absolutely upon its environment by the conscious effort of an imperious will

round this lady for some time all my thoughts had been concentrated. I shall write of her again

at the very start of my un-literary task, already conscious that the words I am setting down

record on the discovered lands the names of those to whom the Expedition owes its being

"But you, Roger? Surely you have married." "No", he replied at length. "No, I have not married"

during his marriage, he was virtually impotent, and only at times was he able to perform as much as ejaculatio praecox

she rejoined the remainder of the passengers, having in her hands a doped handkerchief

only God, the *actus primus*, can move the will to the very act of choosing; if aught else did this, the will would cease to be free

the Government, in a word, should have dealt with illegal acts without asking anyone's leave

his body sways as he weaves in and out, making him a very elusive target to land on with a hard

aircraft in such small police wars as are constantly going on somewhere within the Empire.

1922

I am attempting to evolve a conscious pseudo-symphonic construction toward an abstract beauty

to unrivet the perception from the need, to disentangle art from the practical artifice of life

whose history (which is clearly of a fabulous or symbolical nature) is

a set of doctor's books with colored plates of the insides and pudenda of men and women. I devoured all the volumes, and bits of knowledge from them stuck to me

as the liquid medium by means of which words or characters are recorded upon paper or other fabric as a more or less permanent

slim-waisted man of forty-six with an effeminate voice and taste in flowers, cretonnes, and flappers

easily ascertainable to be unusually fine in other characteristics, is probably "queer" in sex tendency

ladled into his nose sufficient snuff to have doped an ordinary man

felt as though he had been stuffed with clay; his body was bursting, his throat was bursting, his brain was hot mud

the gratification obtained can only relate to the region of the mouth and lips; we therefore call these areas of the body *erotogenic zones*

his galvanometer is registering the production or utilization by the body of adrenalin

prone, weight on elbows, I drank heavily of its perfect blackness. It was icy, talkative, minutely alive

a brain hard as stone, a brain receptive as wax, and a brain unstable as flowing water

all one needs is a pattern, a few scraps of calico, gingham, cretonne or chambray, and some odds and ends of pearl or strand embroidery cotton.

1923

The manufacture of artificial people is a secret process

in shining boots, they stroll about, slim and elegant, twirling swagger sticks

all the flowers in which they tread have supped the essential air whose summer is a-pulse with music

to-morrow the lieutenant is going to bring one of Tolstoi's books to read. Then they will do some music together, she piano and he violin

introduce us to many a secret phase of historical events, and, above all, show

the most sniveling, poltroonish, ignominious, mob of serfs and goose-steppers under one flag

was man in the very first plasm-speck

a bacterium so minute as to be unfilterable through earthenware

the oscillation in the oscillating circuit is then suddenly quenched

a car with the voice of a prehistoric saurian warned him

the bells of thousands of push-cycles

the wheels often got red hot, the shoes sometimes melted

the distinction between sensing and remembering grows fainter, and no absolutely sharp line can be drawn

in the yard of a garage with a specially prepared greasy ground, and afterwards on the rain-sodden surface of a West End square.

1924

THE SCENE represents two drawing-rooms, exact duplicates, furnished alike to the smallest detail. The division line is indicated, towards the back of the stage, by two pianos

he paid for two of the most expensive seats, and placed Madeleine in the one that gave him the best view of her profile

when a pianist articulates a series of muscular innervations

she'll two-time you like she double-crossed me

I'll be damned, hot ziggety damn

as he tore and lifted, she saw through his ragged shirt the swift play under the skin of muscles

whose potency has already been seriously diminished by masturbation

by means of stereoscopic photography they can obtain an impression of a third dimension

I found him taking x-ray pictures of a dog's stomach filled with

a variety of materials used in chemical warfare, as toxic vapours, lachrymators and smoke producers

this "soul" was regarded as similar to the body in form and nature, and as having a quasi-material existence

which presents the problem of the preservation of an independent, creative personality where

a large percentage of young girls do not know of the existence of the vagina

and the *Narrow Way* and the *Wide Way* are varieties of the *Running River.*

1925

On principle I disapprove of writing; on principle I desire

graded "absurdity tests" in which marks were given for detecting and
explaining absurd statements

destroyed by what is commonly known as *the worm* — little six-legged,
white grubs which live inside the wood, devouring it and turning it to

the impression of the printed words on the retina. This sets up an
agitation which we must follow as it goes deeper and deeper

for a time the patient succeeded in bringing her personal wishes, social
aspirations and libidinal needs all under the aegis of the oral erotogenic
zone, in accordance with

The Bee Cell Supporter. A Boon to Womankind. Made from the purest,
softest rubber. Endorsed by the medical profession

in addition to above the following equipment is required: rubber tubing,
1 yard. Adhesive plaster, assorted, 6 reels. Cyanide gauze, 2 lb.
Kruschen salts, 2 bottles

elbow-length sleeves, closely-fitting collars and rougeless faces

for when they came into contact with her heavily beaded eyelashes
they assumed an inky colour, and pursued the rest of their way in slow
black rivulets

but anyone who has watched the way in which newspapers can turn
the public mind to the direction their proprietors desire will realise

there is also a rhythm between transparency at night and expansion of
the pigment-cells by day

the way the fire siren whined when it was dying away

implies that a person has the power of considering the forms and colors
of an object without reference to the object itself

such are the visions which ceaselessly float up, pace beside, put their
faces in front of, the actual thing.

1926

In these days of manifolded information and broadcast amusement

it is well known that (a) different individuals behave differently as regards their own relative evaluation of different coloured lights

the subject regresses to his infantile attitude towards the parent of the opposite

house that, when it was quite complete in his mind, he was some day going to live in

I enter another room in which men are pumping Wagner over telephone wires

ascribed to the medium's thoughts or memories taking visible shape in ectoplasm

too rich and too highly seasoned; it tended to induce those before whom it was spread to

chance to be a mechanical jazz pirouettist or a financial oracle

he drew his revolver and shot once, twice into the ugly black mass. Immediately his anger left him

newspapers were re-appearing in weird type-written or roneo-ed form

can be traced down through links of emotion from the conscious mind into the so-called

smoker of Mexican Loco-weed

throwing back his head in silence, opening his wide mouth and showing his soft pink

strings and a music comes to you, from where you do not know.

1927

Possibly you are thinking of the connection between insanity and phases of the moon

the property here referred to (the quantum property) is the deepest mystery of light

they stroll together amicably, following the doublings and twists of the path, meeting or overtaking other couples and overhearing

the results of the philoprogenitive vigor of a former pastor in that very community

one man slapped him on the back, pump-handled his arm, and roared "Hooray! your Majesty!

nor does he use an endearing phrase to his daughter. The play is a good illustration of the way that the old codes of Japanese chivalry

had to be re-run last week because the electric hare ran too fast

she thought, putting together some of the pictures he had cut out — a refrigerator, a mowing machine, a gentleman in evening dress — children

though small, were too big and heavy to be removed, as the wasps perceived at once

they worked their way in the connective tissue, until they finally came to be beneath the skin on the back, where

the struggle for existence was extremely intense — so severe, indeed, that

those among us who desire to labor at the hazardous business of trying to think hope to

adjust the means of production to the means of consumption

and for me the whole intricate question of method resolves itself not into the power of the writer to bounce the reader.

1928

The grating whine of gramophones excited the ravished silence

on raw-wood shelves were files of paper and blue-books

whose covers turn railway bookstalls into imitations of a cubist flower-bed

metal-green, jewel-green, dawn-green, splashed and flecked with rose, and mooned over with patinas of

varieties of food products for which a reclosure feature is of particular advantage to the consumer

and with perfect judgement in a difficult cross-wind discharged a mail-dropping parachute

connected in a causal chain with the movements of the human body; (b)

this instrument determined the correct moment for the releasing of a bomb by means of a clock-work mechanism

Chicago nor any other community can long endure a peace guaranteed by gunmen

violating the Federal Copyright Law. All parties participating in this will be prosecuted upon their discovery

two thousand lumber-jacks were in town, ham-fisted great fellows with pine needles growing out of their ears

producing work that can be read solely as English poetry, but recapturing the very essence of

hickory is the hardest wood fucking does a woman good it opens her eyes makes her wise and gives her ass exercise

a pineapple was exploded in the building of the Chicago Heights Star.

1929

For technical reasons all is necessarily seen through a young girl's lustrous and youth-blinded eyes

Miss Thong breathed hard, quivered with delight, pressed her hands together and stared and stared

smiled the saurian smile of the sand lizard and basked in the sun

she remembered the smell that rose from the earth in which their roots were lovingly intertwined, a smell of quickening and decay

ill-dressed and unkempt, she rose in a noisy Pentecostal church and cried "I'm tired of this ol' World!

I must seek the night and the cold of its printed stars

milliners' and clothiers' models posturing with waxen gaiety

neat nursemaids perambulating the pink-cheeked babies of the well-to-do

the vital contradiction between the social character of labour and private acquisition

the grafting into men of testicles from apes

I am going to buy a Ford on payments, strike me pink if I don't"

peasant domestic production and artisan production becomes more and more disintegrated

as sometimes, in the playhouse, while pizzicati shimmer, and lights are low. Suddenly

a quick-change artist, an acrobat and the usual red-nosed comedian.

1930

Each generation of mankind inherits an ever-richening treasure of synthetic wisdom from the total human past

in which all the loose ends of the visible world are being caught up into a new mental fabric

evenings he sat in his little log shack back of the hotel drinking paregoric and mumbling

a thin stream of carefully-chosen, watery words

I who am here dissembled proffer my deeds to oblivion, and my love to the posterity of the desert

after dinner he went to the pictures and saw a film about a girl who was constantly undressing and showing her underclothes

"I have put them all in my pocket," she said, with just the faintest disappointment

to suggest that the machinery I have been using upon poetry is going to become increasingly necessary if

events we see are as the pouring of river water into the sea, while events we do not see restore this water back to the river

till we come suddenly on pockets where is nothing loud but us

teleplasmic masses resembling arms and legs

in brightly coloured robes with the word "Wizard" on their conical hats

at Grand Island, opened. The huge monitoring receiving station will not only police the air but will serve as a standard

derived from the idea that thought is a hidden process which it is the aim of the philosopher to penetrate.

1931

Penis, sight of another man's, most dangerous

within its coils lies a disk grooved by a tongue of fire. This is the "Pearl
of the Dragon", symbol of thunder and lightning, and

influence particularly the visual and auditory spheres

damage total. Waves seen on ground surface. Lines of sight and level
distorted. Objects thrown upwards into the air

there is no interrogation in those eyes or in the hands, quiet over

a three-in-one garment, comprising vest, bloomers, and underpants

he sat down himself, when she left the room, overpowered by the very
idea of

the occurrence of emotional elements and pseudoperceptions
(centrally evoked perceptions)

in the complex, involved, manifoldly conditioned "appearances" of this
kaleidoscopic world

a poisonous reptile, called *aranai*, was found in the soup; he opened his
mouth, but before a sound came out of it, Doreen said

heart-stirring, memory-haunting Coty odeurs are what every woman
secretly hopes for

in this manner the head officials of a prosperous company conceived
the idea of putting through the wages books large sums in respect of
fictitious names and "dead" men

all the while writing, or moving swiftly with the pointer of the ouija
board.

1932

Many otherwise respectable readers have, during moments of irritation, an impulse to destroy a book

when this book wrote itself

the turbulent uncertainties of the poet's day-to-day existence blur the reader's mind

the publisher's reader reported that it was worth printing, and offered to publish it on the half-profits system. I had the sense to put it on the fire

this he poked up a little, blew upon it, threw upon the coals some fragments of gum-benjamin or aloes, and a delicious smoke was produced

this we may call its pseudo-intuitive character

nothing more than a sheet of cheese-cloth, which she had swallowed and was able to regurgitate

past the lone copse where poachers set their wires

round and happy among the males and dense with

sources from which the student may draw phrases in common use

form sentences and wonder what they mean

might be formed by a mock marriage of Centrists and Hitlerites

I do not try to pull him back, I only feel the inevitable farawayness

due principally to boredom and the natural outcome of repression and the lack of healthier pursuits.

1933

The student will find in any contemporary textbook of Geology an account of the Noguchi petrograph, which has now made hidden things visible to a depth of

desire to bring the clothed body, and usually though not exclusively the genital region, into close contact with the clothed body of a woman

capitalist and pianist vacillate between rhythmical and analogical accentuation

I watched their curious gestures; the play of their hands, the touch on the cheek, the lips, the breast

from above and underneath it is forever being worked upon by the moving shuttles that go and come and never pause, that rack and shove the fabric on

all the radiation entering the hole will be absorbed by the lampblacked

fragments here selected are rather disjointed, though the beauty of phraseology shows that poetic appreciation

in which the actor (*John*) is the subject and the action (*ran*) the predicate

this young man's total tension of balked dispositions will be eased considerably if in his new environment he can

turn his hydrocephalic head on the pivot of his neck with the slow gravity of the ghost in Punch and Judy

make the famous epigram about there being only two classes of pedestrians — the quick, and the dead

when called to order, he declared that the phrase was a quotation, and that he had really inclosed it between inaudible inverted commas

an improved course of treatment for kleptomania, mental disorders and hookey is being offered at the "Malignant Institute", conducted by "Professor" Boston Allen, negro

"De quickah death, de quickah heaben."

1934

A nation's writers are the voltometers and steam-gauges of that
nation's intellectual life

flashed upon the brain-screen from your own *private* stock of images

the volume of local messages may be affected in a way which does not
reflect changes in business activity by special events, such as
extraordinary weather

roll cumulus or stratocumulus undulatus, appearing in the rear of a
disturbance

the patient really is speaking the truth, and unwittingly the phantastic
lies are distorted expressions of his repressed infantile

dust of exploded beliefs may make a fine sunset

a constipated stool may enter into the creation of a recto-urethral
fistula

that lives as a full-grown female inside a small translucent barrel of the
fire-flame or

pay for it easily on the Chase Time-Payment Plan

natives were already busy wrenching the wire mattresses from the
sofas and unfixing the pivot-chairs from the floor

constructing a geological and meteorological time-scale for the
Southern Hemisphere

we feel the pulse of their rapture beat between intensity of sensuous
vision and its transcendence

regarded as an entirely verifiable mutual property of systems of clocks
in relative motion

an amberized spider with a number of young ones round about her,
and a suggestion of the web.

I began to imagine that I had died and gone back to earth as a

quick motion film of thought

a girl parting her hair in a cool hurry; a family at a Sunday supper
gathered round silver dishes; four people at bridge under a lamp

a salad of lettuce whittled into shoestrings and doped with vinegar and
bacon grease

a hophead who lends another hophead a small quantity of morphine

a man with a high conical head, luminous green flesh, and beard the
colour of pale sea-weed

a treatise on phytotherapy

a sharp variation in a small distance, or in a short time at a fixed point,
in one or more of the atmospheric variables

a sentence that would embody the quiddity of the spectacle

the descending order of female relaxation in the town of Yale

the cleansing of the face under brass taps, the light turning of pages of
manuscript

the million-noted ululation of the night

a struggling young tenor who sings a song of love on the heart-strings
of one woman and the purse-strings of another

my father's voice crying up out of the earth and quicklime where they
stuck him.

1936

The phone rings; a tension is built up and instantly released by
answering the call

the days going by one very much like another

an idea that this is the proper way to work; that cranky ideas, confused
ideas form the best background for artistic creation

where knifed-off slum blocks like stub teeth post around the blank and
roaring mouth of sand

the new script was a complete model of the mechanical process one
performs with it

as if the speed of light, breaking through anastigmatic lenses, can
possibly

profess confidence about the meaning of the writing

but now I can't find it in any dictionary at all

reciting his words by rote in whatever part he plays, and his directors
help him to exercise a lustrous and repulsive

plane trip to Hollywood and a screen test, beside a trophy and reams of
evanescent publicity

the airman wore a two-piece suit of rubberised fabric

an ill-concealed loin cloth all abulge as if with a deep sea catch

precautions were no less thorough to prevent him from returning to
this world to molest the living

where the effigies of the various gods were displayed behind small
sanctuaries.

1937

It would be possible to write a poem unimpeachable as to rational sequence, yet wholly inconsecutive

with the difference between syntactical concepts and the concept that

in wet weather, yellow spore tendrils ooze from these dots

in his emergence to consciousness man rose above the time-stream of sense

in a laminated celluloid model of the human body

longed to wear an evening dress but couldn't because of Psoriasis

it is his custom to invite you to some hotel where he will probably attempt to ply you with liquor

oughta be tried and sentenced tuh six months behind de United States privy house at hard smellin'

he clambered through his skeleton to the place of his skull, and receeded, as if almost in a corporeal ingression to the place where

people are always hearing violins played on the other side of doors and going into rapt attitudes in

feet that move with assurance to the right controls — in Fortune Shoes, your feet move with

neurasthenics, pessimists, cranks and rainbow-chasers

read a poem several times, brood upon it, and next morning find that it had clothed itself from head to foot in music

as we sing: "Skit-skat beety-o! Skit-skat beetyo! Labor is the thing, my lads. Labor is the thing."

1938

The sun shone, having no alternative

over every home in America a grim shadow is cast

and the agent of destruction is the poet

a street accident, an overheard quarrel, a certain note in a voice, a face
coming too close

a man propelling himself through the air by blowing into a box

scanned a vast wilderness of interior Alaska today in search of

my line of thought was: "By Jove, I've lost my memory; what a problem

you are a molecule including various atomic experiences of mine, but

suddenly a country expands an airball in one's

white linen knickers — plus sixes or possibly plus eights, and, pinned to
the front of it, an outsize fraternity pin with more pearls than you'd
care to count

the best snake pearls I ever seen, he'll git you a pearl for each mark
that's there. We're sure going to be rich now"

no matter what he says, someone nods his head and shouts, "amen!

the manly way it gets down to business and shaves you, quick and
close, the first time you put it on your face

left a suicide note to efface his trail and vanished.

1939

It is not the business of philosophers to fit together the results of the scientists in a great jig-saw puzzle, but

a start is made by inserting scissor blades into the cranial cavity and cutting back along each side in turn through the

jitterbug shoe for young men, called "Swingaroo" — plenty swishy with lots of funny sayings printed on the natural color uppers

pearls of knowledge and erudition, gems without price, invaluable carbuncles of sophistry and scholastic science

the function of the activating impurity is to enter the host lattice and produce therein centres of distortion

trepanned by the telepathic acuity of our interacting agitation, I

was sitting in our blue parlour after dinner, intent upon

the manufacture of propaganda — much of it deliberately misleading

nearly all the midgets in the United States were recruited and costumed and given gaily colored wigs and beards to play

silent, jack-booted watchers standing outside frightened houses

the great picture hats made their faces shadowy and mysterious

their quick fingers and their quick minds assure speed and quality of

dictatorship by the combined groups of Electricity, Chemicals, and Iron and Steel

incorporated in your vanilla ice cream by a special fudge ripple attachment as it flows from your continuous freezer.

1940

Abstractish figures with shelter background. Disintegration — of
bomber of person of machine

as quartz increases the quartzose schists grade to schistose quartzites

the back room becomes drabber and dingier in the gray daylight that
comes from the street windows, off right, and what light can penetrate
the grime

points, and another day prepares for heat and

a poetic statement is a quasi-assertible relation between plurisigns. I
say "quasi-assertible" because

the purr of a waterfall rose and sank with the wind

past the window, towns popped up, announced their names with a
placarded station momentarily thrown on the screen

now the sky turns hostile. Around us searchlights pry into thin clouds

change the course of mighty rivers, bend steel with his bare hands, and
who — disguised as

the workers were sick of Hitler and even more sick of having to drink
"Ersatz" coffee and wear shoes of petrified silk and blouses of wood
pulp

throughout intra-uterine life the head is always very large in
proportion to

beautiful bodies, think of music, art, poetry — these are the mere first
intimations of how the

crack in the tea-cup opens a lane to the land of the dead

one event is, as it were, "glued" to another.

1941

Physical terror is, in the long run, secondary to the job of winning the minds and feelings of the masses to a set of

tin hats and rifles slung over the shoulder. My shadow on the whitened inner wall was like a figure on a war memorial

the amnesia was already less marked, and autopsychic orientation

agreed to hand over to Germany a number of political and racial refugees

DEAD STUDIO: studio having short reverberation time and giving, therefore, a dull acoustic effect

where the lost souls are tortured

in the torsion of the engined firmament

pushing the clouds around, dead

at one time they were prevented from burying their dead until

we are cemeteries where lie sleeping the millions of men who bear our name

what is truth? Balls. What is love? Shite. What is God? Bugger. Ah, but what is beauty?

a window opening upon a starlit canal with a great drooping church, weighed down

at once, from motor-car lamps, windows and skylights, a succession of Morse Vs twinkled in reply

and the dead begin from their dark to sing in my sleep.

1942

The pattern in which wars are made

is a pattern of timeless moments

we are, along the time coordinate, linking up phenomena

in the direction of our fear

listeners to these programs often give wide currency, either casually or
with ulterior purpose, to

problems of the natures of ideas, *ideata*, and the things cognized,
pseudo-cognized, mistaken, doubted, or fancied

you know your ownself how looking back always slows people up

won't have enough time to realize he is about to become a victim of an
American pioneer, the name of the

girl had a gun, and told McNaughton: "You're a two-timer and no
good. I'm going to kill you"

he is conscious not only of the feelings but of the linguistic activity, and
works at performing this activity as well as he can

banged his coffee cup down. "You want to hire a private eye, say so,
and just leave out all the innuendoes"

can be traced to definite action on the part of those on board the
warship in directing the course of the vessel in order to carry out the
warlike operation

whose spirit is a wet sack flapping about the knees of time

for the bigger experiences need time, perhaps a long time, before we can
make poetry of them.

1943

She boarded the eastbound bus at Mattoon, and settled her ample proportions into the reclining seat next to me

the froggy gloss on her tight skin besprinkled with brown

just above the brown line of the horizon, faint as a watermark on pale blue paper, was the tracery of the mountains

on the rubberneck wagons the fellow with the megaphone would point it out and

spit would run out of her mouth and she would start out in a low grumbling voice and gradually get to talking as loud as her throat could stand it

she thought that she was only interested in duplicating a dream, but in doing so she necessarily became the complete victim of

an "Aerocar" intended primarily as a family automobile. For weekend flying trips, it dons wings in your garage and skims through the air

by doubling the fist and allowing the tip of the thumb to protrude between the index and the middle finger, or the gesture may be

designed by the Company's architects office, in order to assist in solving the wartime problem of enabling passengers to obtain a cup of tea

what is thus rationalized into a pseudo-opposition turns out, as it so often happens, to be

circular so that visitors may see the fine mountain and lake views in all directions

at which pathological investigations and research on seminology could be undertaken

concerned here only with the vibration of elastic bodies and elastically coupled mechanical systems

sun still shines practically every day of the year, regardless of Hitler and Hirohito. So come — re energize for the post-war jobs ahead.

1944

Moral questions often present in a Babel of tongues, where

the clairovoyante that evening was good, but it was the speaker who claimed

the peculiar circumstances of his melodramatic career remained a subject of speculation for the best part of a century

this man, thought Vernier, has a baby's faith in himself, and a baby's hatred of strangers

he had in some fashion discovered that there were some ways in which to be human was utterly dismal, and all his life was given to

make larger and larger areas of his otherwise private experience available to other men

the earth, the universe, this planet. Any place that's large

all the pieces of road that I remembered so well, only now I was being driven in a

street car or to be able to walk into a drug store and plunk down the cash for a chocolate soda or coca cola

to a living God who reveals himself not merely in external nature or in the operations of our minds, but on particular historical occasions

our memories are card-indexes consulted, and then put back in disorder by authorities whom we do not control

for reasons of security, since they may throw light on the total numbers employed and so upon the numbers and equipment of the Armed Forces

let him read a second time and reflect how many of the passages first taken as literal truths are really metaphors

which make the individuals as far as possible act spontaneously in the way the planner wants.

1945

What is requisite of theories incorporated in poems is not that they be true, but that they be pronounced by a character who evinces a sincere attitude

the idea underlying one important part of the mechanism came to him in a dream

a girl stroked its keys and it emitted recognizable speech

in which a constant rate of motion is adjusted by mechanical means. Operator adjusts an error voltage

with the adrenal courage of the tiger

in abstract understanding, without adoration, he puts colors on canvas, a picture of the universe in which

the side car, the monkey gland, the fallen angel, the serpent's tooth, the stinger, the six whispers

which, prior to 1939, had been relegated to the lingual dustheap, suddenly became

but the endless repetition of zero

apply a thin layer of Prussian blue or white lead to one of the suspected parts or to a cartridge in order that a more visible mark will

have made possible the rise of those reactionary movements which have tried, and still try, to overthrow civilization and

your letter found me last night when I came in off the piss: in point of fact I

do not find this prose meaning in any of the poem's dark corners. The individual quality of the poem can, it is true, be

the attack which now, from so many sides, is being made upon the life of human reason.

1946

Shyly things say what they mean

the iceberg cuts its facets from within

the mother whose sexual needs are not met may release her tensions by

cramming it into the pollen chambers with her tongue

and began to rain in the face like a professional mourner

the nebulous blur of her thoughts hardened. She said, and her voice
was almost panic-stricked

concepts do not resemble the objects they are concepts of, but

they have already buried four hundred Moslem heroes with their
swords whose task it will be to defend the Mosque of Omar against a

surgeon, noting a slight rise in temperature, wondered, "Is it post-
operative pneumonia?" Within an hour the radiologist developed a
chest X-ray

the panel and plates of the tube became red hot and appeared to absorb
the Xenon present in the tube thus

the mycelium from within the shoot tissues appeared at the outer
surface and burst through the epidermis to form pustules

having isolated our problem, "How shall I choose?" from "How have I
chosen in the past?" and "Which action is right?" we must

the books in all their thousand smell sleepily of cellar

with their outward expression in events he is concerned only in so far
as these reveal to him the thoughts of which he is in search.

1947

Consider now what happens to the children who escape death in infancy

the vibration of a pneumatic tool, particularly after prolonged use, affects the blood vessels of the hand, frequently impairing the circulation and

to see how folks will miss you, stick your finger in the pond, then pull it out and look at the hole

four hundred and four missing women were either traced or excluded during the weeks which followed

effected no change in the position of things as they are

death rate is the same here as elsewhere — one death for every inhabitant

a clicking becomes audible from the telephone, steady and rasping

in which the spermatids, still enclosed in cysts, are converted into *spermatozoa*; and break through the cyst wall by lashing movements of

sixteen assorted "queens" of such things as spring, sports, tomatoland, sauerkraut, and others

groveled in the dust of a backwoods clearing in convulsive rites which bid the faithful handle serpents to confirm their salvation, baptized by "burial" beneath

feeding grounds not only for numerous springtails and millipedes, but also for the carnivorous beetles, spiders and pseudo-scorpions which prey upon them

inclined to accept for informal usage was in place of were in conditions of doubt

due to the geometrical interference of the many small roughnesses on the two rubbing surfaces

experienced one of the keenest pleasures, the pleasure of recognition: they was themselves, their neighbours, their own shores.

1948

A medical practitioner must notify the Medical Officer of Health of his district of the occurence of any of the following in his practice: membranous croup, erysipelas, enteric fever, relapsing fever, glanders, farcy, cerebrospinal fever, hydrophobia

reversible liquefaction of any gelated regions of the protoplasm

heterosexual prostitution, variant techniques, anal coitus, anilinctus, flagellation, masochism, scatology, voyeurism

a person who drives a car blindfolded supposedly under the psychic influence of another person

armaments manufacturers, S.S. men accused of racial crimes

a 74-year old ex-schoolteacher, the venerable and bearded man below, the duly accredited candidate of the Vegetarian party

the schools of thecosome pteropods with which they are always found

a huge time-eaten barrel organ that produces martial-sounding dances with missing notes, clanging bells, and queer, mechanical birdcalls

a sea of dragomen, panders, peddlers, mendicants, tumblers, fakirs, and assorted mountebanks

the Ravennese Exarchate

certain fixed and astral values; things like character and family and the Episcopal Church

the wondrous hail, the curse of the locust, and modern bombs

a material, external, independent world

YOU ... and the man you love ... your home ... your table ... your Community, it's a dream-come-true, *for keeps!*

1949

An agent possesses a Privileged Access to the so-called springs of his own

Pinkertons fighting pitched and bloody battles with Carnegie Steel strikers

colours normally show lowlands in greens, passing into browns for highland

we look at a ravaged face and reconstruct the grief and shock that laid those lines down

his record dated back to 1937 and included seven different types of crime including

the use of Hymns Ancient or Modern in industrial disputes, a profanation of a sacred book

after reading the book I built an orgone accumulator, and the gimmick really works

contemporary neurology explains the sudden changes in emotional behaviour as a release from cortical control of the

orifice that is pouring forth secretion while the doubtful side is re-inspected

discovered about a dozen inscriptions written in a previously unknown syllabic script

Pluscold and *doublepluscold* meant, respectively, "very cold" and "superlatively cold"

and on the back of the door at Cesena are, or were, still the intitials *Joli quart d'heure*

the mere sight of which caused a laciniate shiver to branch from my spine like nocturnal lightning

I gaze at the sentence in wonder, realising what a long journey I have to go before I reach his death.

1950

A body is weightless as soon as it is allowed to move freely under the influence of gravity and of its own inertia

the Popes proceeded to transfer thousands of bodies to

the spectral region where efficient luminescence emission is to be produced

where almost all the altars found are covered with the sign of the Day God Ahau

their world has returned to what they think the whole world ought to be: water

every tiny runlet and burn was rushing in spate down towards the sea

ejected from their source at very high velocities, perhaps 5,000 miles a second, in all directions

to "make life less unnatural" aboard submarines, such as overheads painted to resemble

the erotising effect of the coitus *a posteriori*

whose porosity enables paraffin-oil or other suitable heavy oils to be slowly combusted

with the shimmer and the smell, the peculiar force of money, the promise of it

as twelve separate Soviet air armies totalling over 100 air divisions equipped with more than 10,000 planes were flung in

with my money to outfit a lugger to dredge for pearl shell and trepang off the

intricate evasions of as, in things seen and unseen, created from nothingness.

1951

I lay in my bed in the ward of the Hospital dominated above all by

childhood memories we are both trying to recover and recover from

gathered together from such sources as have by accident been available
to me, and to make a work out of these mixed

sheets of typewritten manuscript, with words scrawled out and new
lines scrawled in

just care about the words. Dwell on them lovingly

crisp and radiant, with labels dead white and perfect, with spines sound
and round and flawless at the edge

push-buttoned, refrigerated, motorized and armed like

treaties of reciprocity and international agreements woven around the
earth that makes it possible for the citizen to take his legal status with

these ruthless, paste-faced automatons in high-shouldered jackets
whom or which

manifolded themselves upon the air between earth and heaven like
falling leaves and falling snow

Pink Ladies, Honolulu cocktails and créme de menthe highballs, they
would regard as an insult

what did appal them were the wild cats in the kitchen, glaring out from
the cold blackness over the extinct ranges, these Maenads seemed to be

the sex act, which leaves them headachy, anticlimactic, and burdened
with the fact that they

expect to have the world's greatest radar wall in operation across
western Europe by mid-1952.

1952

Complex spits are those which send out branches during growth

ray-diagrams are used to illustrate aspects of the sphere of

penny-arcade tableaux called "What the Butler Saw Through the Keyhole", sighting off lickerishly at

a comic picture, it was that of Punch, and made believe in its possession of divine attributes

his rather ectoplasmic voice effused itself into Cathy's ear

she moistened her lips with a little pointed tongue

the rasp of it across his skin was the last thing he clearly remembered

and the sinister rustling of Natural Sciences Part ll men being instructed in the use of secret codes

they rejected his ricky-ticky beat with distaste

by dropping a germ bomb which looks just like an ordinary bomb, but is filled with germ-laden insects; (2) by dropping insects in paperboard containers which will break open on contact with

the underworld, which was a place of incineration — not punishment

every time he reaches a high point. He'll start leaving out punctuation and running his words together and

about five o'clock he will start talking about going into a quiet place and having a couple of quick

walls between the closely adpressed organs break down followed by a mingling of the protoplasm.

1953

I was crosssing the rainbow bridge from reality to dream

made in lengths of about four inches wide invisibly joined with

coconut shies and rifle galleries, Aunt Sallies and penny-rollers, seemed like soldiers after a long battle

de moon sorta mellow ovuh de ya'd

evening would remain as a pin-point of light which she would still see when, as an old woman by some fireside, she looked back along the

roofs of reinforced wood wool with a half-inch screed and ply-felt finish

which is a dead thing though it once had aesthetic life in the artist's mind

you're living a magnificently casual life in mid-century America. Your clothes reflect it; your home is gracious and glass-walled

unfortunately, in the fresco within the church the halo of the Madonna has been recently over-gilded

opposite the agent, separated by an intervening screen with a small square hole in it, sat an experimenter with in front of her five cards

what makes a *perpetuum mobile* of this yearning for the renovation of life is nothing but the calamity that between one's misty ego and one's predecessors' ego there is interpolated a pseudo-ego

one might (using the language of chemistry) call this picture a proposition-radical

heat for 2-4 hours under a reflux condenser in isopropanol containing excess aluminium isopropoxide

then, suddenly, the bison painted on the cave wall.

1954

In the little pink-eyed cottage next to the untertaker's, lie, alone, the seventeen snoring gentle stone of

the duchess, lying on the chaise-longue under the window; she was swathed like a mummy in yards of cyclamen chiffon trimmed with marabout

an enamel basin at her feet is filled, usually to overflowing, with cigarette ends

transparently there, in the word-bin, wrapped each in cellophane, ready made for sense-making (in sentences)

contained in the illustrative quotations which are not only numerous but so arranged that their relation

Claude gave her money, a regular allowance. It was always spent before the end of the quarter on gin and betting

the servant who fetches the dish of *refis* shall receive from the hand of her mistress one mouthful of it, no more

she hopefully asked me to draw a map of her stomach, giving me minute instructions, and clapping my hand to the place

the areas of rarefaction within the opacification of the liver begin to be much more apparent

explained phylogenetically as marriage by capture and psychologically as the sexual desire to be overmastered

where men have always found the raw materials of myth and

recounted her husband's activities, the things he had done thus far, the things that still remained to be done

as she read on, she had the impression of meeting a ghostly, ectoplasmic regurgitation by reality of

power out of the earth and spread like fine root-threads in the ground.

1955

Did the spring grass heal winter's ravages?

the experience had a human content, which the earlier, solitary experience, with its Other Worldly quality

played on the erotogenic zones of the

meat, fat, and suet, in making sausage, scrapple, and other meat concoctions

respondents used somewhat facetious synonyms for the area spanked

and he may fear secretly that his adopted parents might some day give him up to

fight communism with Truth Dollars

buried them in quicklime, so that there was nothing left of them

he said that radioactive polonium, selenium and antimony have been studied as possible weapons for controlling worm parasites

he had had a dream that he considered foolish and not worth

transmitting via Marine telephone by an Associated Press correspondent, who has been marooned by bad weather atop the Texas radar island

burning for the ancient heavenly connection to the starry dynamo in the machinery of night

but when the apellant denied that he had ever been in Middleton, where the Will Jones mentioned in the rap sheet had been picked up, the district attorney made pretense that he was having the temerity to deny

that he tried to perform fellatio on a male dog can be construed as evidence of latent homosexuality associated with oral eroticism.

1956

The 6000 ton radar island is the first in a circle of outer warning stations

occupies the exact site of the original building and is the same in every detail

at night in the deep and dead time, he hears again the soft scraap of his curette against the uterus wall in a room that holds no other sound

this continuous activity of God is not to be thought of as if it were the insertion of creatures into a time-flow which existed antecedently to

the helicar, a combination of automobile and helicopter

"But Mr. Elephant hasn't been near the canvas!" "Amazing! Surrealists try to paint without thinking, but this is painting without painting!"

Fiona thought hard of a negro Staff-Sergeant whom she had once seen throwing the whole of the University Jazz Club into ecstasy with an erotic and protracted paradiddle

there was some excitement, and "Vote Auden" was chalked up on the walls of New College

the same night, on the old horn gramophone I heard some amateur's recording of the old poet reciting the lines which begin

the ease of loading, the push-button starting, the constant filtering of the water!

one of his most beautiful poems pictures his poignant sensations as he comes from a quiet hour within dim, organ-haunted shadows

he thought he shouldn't have poll-parrotted his life away in humbug and

stood ready to scramble aircraft aloft to intercept any unidentified planes

thus scoring tremendous results in training our people in immeasurable love for the country as well as in optimism for our future.

1957

It is the aim of the ultraviolet television color-transmitting microscope
to overcome these drawbacks by providing

a machine that can be used in any one of a finite number of different
internal states. Any language

pertaining to, or transmitting electricity, or electrifying in the senses of
thrilling, exciting or charged

by a comparison of their experienced and expected pleasures and pains
in this quasi-mathematical manner

may be able to "hear everything going on" through the thin party-wall

Oh Aunty! What a funny place to keep the hairbrush

"listen, Jazz-bo," she said, "I know your mom a lot better than you do.
She might let you wheedle the old man, but you can bet your shaggy
fins

rarely, in boys, the anterior inferior spine of the ilium may be pulled off
by a violent contraction

with his paint-loaded brush, and an emphasis on the freedom of the
creative act itself and sensitivity towards the actual materials

was appealing, in other words, to the germ of the self, to the being who
would eventually outgrow

the statistical effects of independent rectilinear movements of
molecules

I could not imagine him unless he had enough being to stand as the
correlate-term in this postulated relation of being imagined by me

when discharge is about to occur, the capsule becomes somewhat
plumper and the coiled thread emerges at such speed that its
movement cannot be followed by the eye

is kept at atmospheric temperature until it reaches a pathologist
experienced in seminology.

1958

Radar stations at sea picked up blips suggesting that an air armada was flying at 2,000 mph towards

the ignorant and the pretentious, the sockless hipsters out for a fast buck or a

collection of examples and *ad oculos* demonstrations of types of human conduct

I felt my nostrils flare like a stud's at the nubby tight sex of them, flustered and pink-scrubbed

what the comprehension effect may be it is difficult to tell for this effect is hidden away inside the organism

matter itself, far from being the means by which we can know the essence of things, is the cause of nothing

the property store, which is also used as a stage, is made up of ply-faced stud frame on light metal supports and is coloured in

all manner of particularizations to stay the pocky moon

I looked across at the ring of faces round him: they were all rapt with attention and pleasure

he will chew leaves, roll quid in caustic ash and then pass it from man to man for a relaxing chew

the mighty throbbing heart of London life stood still. The only sound was a flutter of wings by many pigeons startled by this

blood-and-sex daydream spattered with frankly magic forces whose operation is left deliberately vague

as for the nude dancer, she supplied details of the private lives and sexual eccentricities of the Defence Minister

forms the basis of storage into which information can be written, and from which it can be recovered.

1959

The boy sat by the lake edge. Ply on ply, night bound the floating images of things

images would rise in chimerical visitations and

ganglionic patterns preserved the record of the stream of consciousness

with sufficient computational speed to make use of machine-learning

there is more here than we can say: prismatic lights, prismatic smells, something that sets one's teeth on edge

periodically expanded and contracted, like a kind of pulsating jellyfish

pulsific rhythms, syncopated accompaniments

a nice clean unusual noise from vibraharp, electric guitar, a piano and a bass-viol

inside, the paintings on the walls shifted from imitation Matisse to pseudo-Italian Renaissance

overhead the sky was tight as rawhide

full of fishy winds, trolley buses, girls like plethoric sausages

extracts of fish scales or a mixture of salts which give the shampoo — not the hair — a silky look

faint rays coming from over the edge of the visible disk which seem to indicate ray-centres on the averted side

these fierce & airy occupations, and love, raved away so many of Henry's years.

1960

It is well known that opalinids parasitizing the recta of Amphibia multiply asexually by binary fission

as the nerve called the recurrent nerve passes beneath the brain to

the long white forenoons of childhood, as I lay ill or convalescent, wafting up through the muted sounds of traffic, footsteps, voices

indifferent in some degree to a physical time order, which of course raises

American children almost constantly under the lash of time

the electric, see, and the car and the good water, and the you know, the proper W.C.

as this apparatus is virtually closed except for the groove in the cork of C, it is also convenient for the distillation of pungent and lachrymatory materials

but first, since I was only six, and of wayward temper, they took me by a roundabout route to the meatbutcher's

root-pale her meager frame

she loved the Pitysake she called her son

a sexually uncommitted youth with large, well-cared-for hands, a pissy smile

who had first been convicted before the age of 12

for his presumtuousness in dying before the time divinely set for him and sends him back into the world of men

a man travels through time, leaving behind him a lengthening trail of diapers and dinnerjackets.

1961

The functioning of the brain depends on physical nourishment of the hereditary

storage space, containing old pinochle tournament charts and pool tables

in five brilliant variations propped sassily among the bold webbed

loops and whorls of evolving little worlds

science merely provides the opportunity for tales of action that

will knock a motorblock off its mounts, destroy a small tree, and disembowel a boar

such an impetus in muscle growth that one can describe the results with that over-worked but very appropriate word

I have never taken a drink to improve my appetite, ward off a cold, or get a good night's sleep. I drink with the honourable intention of

travel through the "plasma" of protons and electrons outside

a cheeky 17, bejeaned and homeless, a coffee-bar waif who sleeps on a caff floor

her coat was a rich amber colour, and her piercing, moody eyes a lovely leaf green

and even had the sound of her dress and stick been audible there would have been the usual

flame-tipped, searing, destroying arrow of Eros; O bliss of the end

afterwards, the Royal Greenwich observatory distributes time to the Post Office.

1962

The poem, from begining to end, will offer the careful, cautious, logically-minded reader a succession of

those areas of life which may have remained immune to the cancer of pseudo-eventfulness

the small world of the car plunged through the deep fields of the night

twenty-eight men aboard a damaged radar tower foundered down seventy miles

into the computer field to determine the best methods for introducing a further stage in the automation of the control procedure

complained through his solicitor that police radar speed traps were "un-British" when he was fined £10 for

the genteel hipster hero it accompanied, and with its reed memories and assertive, five-piece, rhythm section backing, it

almost eliminates squeal when cornering

with the added ability to weep, or lacrimate, which is an excessive outpouring of the lacrimal gland

the electronic eye now reinvents after interiorizing the unified field of electric all-at-onceness

almost retires defeated when it tries to report on the abstraction-process involved in using language at all

3 days later, an Elmquist internal pacemaker was inserted in the left rectus sheath, and its electrode was sutured to the ventricular myocardium

the Eternal Recurrence of all things — including himself

does not invalidate the statement in the text, if "definition" is given a constant meaning.

1963

The Manifold of Events is regarded as comprised of a great many outputs from past processes which serve as inputs to present processes that will, in turn, generate outputs to serve as inputs to future

translation of neuro-behavioral functions characteristic of living organisms into electronic, electro-chemical, or electro-mechanical analogs of

the pollution entering our waterways

the imprint of a dog's paws, the beaded tracks of a wagtail

the "raspberry tip", a disc made to look like a quarter but bearing the inscription "zero cents — exactly the value of your service"

"plus-men" capable of reading a wine-list and opening doors for ladies

an electronic "robot" man-handled on its way to its new home in a room on the second floor

the British Museum's "private case" of subversive and erotic literature

air-permeable PVC coated fabrics for upholstered furniture

the "rainbow bomb", so-called because of the beautiful artificial aurora which its explosions created

arbitrary postulates, e.g. cognitively meaningless sentences of a metaphysical pseudo-theory

a piece for Twelve Radios that is performed by turning each to a different

eschatological wisdom, of mystical psychology and theurgic power hidden under a veil of breathless utterances

thus postponing the "crisis of capitalism".

1964

Turning it over, considering, like a madman Henry put forth a book.
No harm resulted from this

all he wanted was an objective recital of events and her own
impressions as a psychiatrist

consisted of everything I should delete from my novel in order to
make it

authenticate even further the self-evident intention of the author to
tell the simple autobiographical truth about his hidden sexual history

imprisoned in a "refractory ward", his control over environment
shrivels

his only refuge was the W.C., where the disinfectant camphor balls
dwindled in the green trough of the urinal, and old men came

continually changing, depending on body-feelings and dominant
emotions

a balance that is sometimes neglected in the *furor poeticus* of textual
speculation

the viewer of the TV mosaic, with technical control of the image,
unconsciously re-configures the dots into an abstract work of art

thoughts and speech became completely uncoordinated, and she had

a pseudo-machine and programs could be written which dealt only
with this pseudo-machine

a great variety of person-tense-aspect prefixes are available to the
speaker of

a verbal homage — unsolicited, naturally — from the male pedestrian
to the beauty and grace of the woman who passes

the pendulous "apron" of fat hanging down from the abdominal wall.

1965

The declaration of war is just one of a series of legal and quasi-legal measures which have a role in

the copulatory movements of a male mantis involving the twisting of his abdomen, movement of his genitalia and deposition of his spermatophore

surveyed the following year by a pleiad of active, enthusiastic entomologists

year by year life lays down another layer of remains for tomorrow

for a buck you could get what you wanted, how you wanted it, sunnyside up or poached, any age including

the earth a turbine storing sexual energy under their skyscrapers with their time on top tickertape time tick tick

I never found in his tomes a surmise concerning even a guessed reason for such constant penile stimulation

set her going like a fat gold watch

which is wholly artificial, made in an engineering workshop, operated either by mechanical pseudomuscles or by twitch stimuli

all over the city, she saw scratched on the back of a seat, shining for her in the brilliant smoky interior, the post horn with the legend

desperate graduate, young wife 7 months pregnant, seeks semi- or unfurn. flat London area. Max £6 10s. Phone after 6pm

never killed anyone for land or for anything that could be described as plentifying myself

once broke off from his loud, lusty and lewd songs to admonish an astonished old man: "I've told yeh once, an' I'll tell you no more, keep away from my granny"

the remains of his smile still lingering about his lips like crumbs left over from a cold snack.

1966

In the quasi-experience of mysticism we experience what the point of everything is

a difficult text which, even if complete, would not allow us to "aha" until after

he took out his portable ink block and wrote the poem down by the light of a holy lantern

he took a drink from the flask, wiped his sooty face with the back of his hand, and returned the liquor to me. Then with a great belch he resumed

in any event, some radio stations have banned the record because the song is an obvious paean to the joys of smoking pot. A rainy-day woman is

adjoint, unjoint, disjoint, anoint, appoint, standpoint, repoint, West Point, viewpoint, dry point

had taken amphetamines in very large amounts, having ingested the contents of nasal inhalers

I'm a sex maniac. Jesus never fails [Signed]

one who expresses his soul-stirrings upon lavatory walls

now pursues adventure in city streets. He challenges schools and recreation-workers to

beware of the (dog) mess on the pavement

might say "I see *Woman* about twice a week" meaning that she goes to a friend's house about twice a week and usually picks up *Woman* while she is there

a reduced and visibly inexperienced cohort of Vietnick demonstrators — bearded, mini-skirted or just plain PV-seedy — outnumbered by journalists and cameramen

may lack their enemies' jungle skill, but the rapid availability of firepower and heliborne mobility have tipped the scales in their favor.

1967

Descriptive phrases such as "I really laid some pipe last night" tend to replace the more specific, denotative labels for intercourse

so I kept Maxine's three younger brothers outside while Teddy slipped the meat to her in the bedroom

wearing only three blinking lights over appropriate sections of her considerable anatomy

this computer can do the work of a thousand men in two seconds

the few words she does speak are genuine hieroglyphs of the inner world of Love and of the higher cognition revealed in the intuition of

a silkworm is visible crawling up the inside of her thigh. Far from protesting the sensation it plainly is causing, she is using

an ant, exploring my disturbance of his polis, enters my head through a nostril

cortical train of spikes shows little or no change in size

he seems to hear around the core of every word the totality of its overtones and undertones

this is to be regarded as mere pathoplastic colouring and the state as one of pseudo-possession only

houses an elaborate masturbation machine that the user operates with a foot pedal

may turn out that man will prefer "ideating" with a machine to "ideating" with his human colleagues

consisting of twelve 30kc tape decks, a high speed printer, a paper-tape reader, and

increased single unit activity in the visual core, increased brain flow temperature, and increased cortical blood flow.

1968

It is not evident that any responsible figure in the Eastern or Western worlds has a clue to the erosion of human identity that follows upon the

drugs known as "rainbow" pills because of the various colors of the

whole other world that LSD opened your mind to

involves a projected perceptual-like image, but one in which the person concerned recognizes the subjective nature of the

wide-eyed, searching appearance of the eyes, called "radar-like gaze"

another person may respond to the same stimulus with a marked increase in palmar sweating

he observed with revulsion as he wiped his wet hand against the chintzed chair arm

he said that one should act as if events recurred; as if what happened to one once went on happening for ever

as the drum gathers momentum riders are flung against the walls and there they stick while

all disease, whether it be physical or emotional, appears to have its time-cycles

a clock that, on being tapped, swings from four o'clock to some other hour, and then on being tapped again, shows

that the probability of eventual return after N steps is unity also, which cannot therefore be true for

bloodied ends of the umbilical Billy takes and wraps up in a poem I had made that

makes stasis, or the absense of further continuation, the most probable succeeding event.

1969

If one considers how difficult it is to carry on two conversations simultaneously, one may appreciate the problems of multiple simultaneous interpersonal perception that can arise in even a small-scale orgy

random sequences of scenes, trivial or tragic, viatic or static, fantastic or familiar

as shown in figure 6, a ram generates fluid pressure in the cylinder on the left, which is linked by the augmenting punch to the extrusion container on the right

generate digital transients that caused the abort guidance to send false

theatrical representations of both a mystery play and a family reunion attended not only by the living but by ancestral

jaw relationship so than an intermittent muscle pull from the lower jaw transmits pressure to the teeth, thereby producing tooth movement

others used a soap substitute composed of balls of hog's dung in lye made with wood ashes and chamber-pot water

comets or shooting stars were also seen, and the rocks of Tita not only rumbled but actually threw out some ashes. Other rain rocks "spoke words"

the intravehicular space suit consists of: fecal containment subsystem, constant wear garment

the energy flux associated with a given point on a wave front

due to the stress of reentry, was observed in the urine of the Russian astronauts Komarov, Feoktisov, and Yegorov

on weakly structured, non-cohesive soils with a sparse plant-cover rainsplash erosion can cause detachment and downslope transportation of the loosened

youth keeps the foamrubber waterfall from falling, makes the falling flesh stand firm

with champagne featuring as a substitute for the primitive sacrificial blood.

1970

It would seem that, as the date of the Rapture draws near, humanity is becoming exceedingly space-conscious

in the centre of the profitless lawn a pitiful tube squirts water to a height of a couple of feet

brown roots growing through split blonde hair

styles, piled and shellacked and swirled and horned, filled me with

sensory feedback in the form of response-produced kinesthetic and proprioceptive cues

computed from an unpublished re-classification of the 1895 and 1914 Argentine Census prepared for the Institute of Sociology

containing a record number of typographical errors made by an over-stimulated compositor

sheer drudgery threatened to overwhelm them unless they used machine-assisted information handling

testifies to the merely historical, transitory character of the capitalist mode of production

his thick lips are pursed forward, a little of the pink flesh inside exposed

had these little pin-pricky eyes and I said to myself, shit man!

reckless eyeballing, looking with desire at "forbidden" persons

you can still get away with a small drawing from the blue or pink period, before

my agony rainbowed to ecstasy.

1971

The sentiments resonated by a social theory provide an immediate but privatized

dolly who was obviously after a good time, pumped a few grogs into her, and we left the hotel

she was an eroticist of the first order!

only a body, or something very like a body, can resemble a body in respect of bodyhood and

a way of continuing to exist which does not imply identity through time

expectoration has occurred during at least three consecutive days during at least three consecutive months for more than two successive years

such cyclic stresses exist wherever the fastened members move or vibrate. When the fluctuating stress approaches or exceeds actual bolt tension

he is threatened with self-extinction by two tiny bits of matter — the atom and the fertilised human ovum

takes plaster-casts of their erect genitals so that these effigies can be touched later at leisure

visited each of the Hash producing countries, and to me it seems that the quality of high always reflects

unusual lore and amazing insights into number words and the universal concepts they represent

varying in length from about three to more than twelve inches, into which the penis is inserted

the angle of the dangle and the heat of the meat varies in direct ratio to the mass of the ass

each of which releases a less energetic photon than the original X-ray.

1972

The next morning was dull and he woke to the racket of rain on his iron roof

in the form of droplets of appreciable size such that their individual impact on surfaces is perceptible

properties which affect it are the volumetric content of electrolyte (water content) and its tortuosity, electrolyte concentration, and

slightly rasping as if it had once been ruined by a fit of inordinate demonic laughter

into his life and villa moves the external present in the form of Jill, a rich moonchild on the run from a mother in Connecticut and a pusher in New York

with a sacred glossolalic name for Jesus she would not disclose to me

so I was naturally elated. I galloped through the cash-book and bank reconciliation, then asked for the minute book to get background

as people, the three characters have no personal quiddity, no individual tincture, no spice or smack of their own

the camera sees them — their skin — as harsh, faded, and porous

for it was based on the idea that every culture has its period of youth, only to terminate in decrepitude, petrifaction, what Spengler called

preliminary data for the design of languages for person-machine voice communication

she followed it all in raw movies and magazines, in parks, once, and once on a beach she spied a couple

put up Jesus posters, wear Jesus buttons, and emblazon their car bumpers with stickers that say "Honk if you love Jesus"

the droplet levitation technique has opened up new possibilities for studying the liquid state that we are now exploring.

1973

We, with our excellent childhood radar, always sensed the context even if we missed the words

equipment includes a toilet draincap from Bradley Engineering and "racking and elfin cases" from Cementation Muffelite

helps to remove creep noise from stress relaxation in the

mannequins' dresses, over their cold unnippled breasts and up their fused and icy thighs

very carefully remove the belly of the instrument to be reproduced

"Lights, please". He switched them on, pivoting the 1,000-watt quart-iodine beams onto

a cold, artistic nobility, more permanent than the rain-corrupted stone in the open spaces where our memorials stand

took a minute to get her hand to turn on the light, for she was so racked with a kind of chill, which made her jaws click together like bare bones

doubled over the radar repeater and tracked the range pips

saw a brightly-coloured bus outraging the conventions of traffic, touring the highways like a great itinerant carnival

consisting of the central figure of Christ surrounded by twelve Apostle sculptures, all hand-carved of best quality white Ravaccione (Carrara) statuary marble (used extensively by

the plaster baby, the oxen frosted with gold leaf and the human-eyed sheep

a quasiphotograph of Christ produced by the radiance of the resurrection

with a "soul rush" of blissed-out young pilgrims heading for the Western Mecca of the Most Important Movement in the History of Mankind.

1974

From the very first an image is not the indication of something other than itself, but the pseudopresence of the thing it contains

Quiet World contains special calming and relieving ingredients

reciprocating screw injection moulding machines

"anatomy lessons" or "illustrated" discussions on the respective merits of Swedish and Japanese bathing facilities

as the distance from the skin increases, the air molecules participate more and more in the general movement of the air over the surface, and finally

say things like "Meet me up in your room in 10 minutes with a whip and a prune danish"

four children, a disused railway line, a time-slip to an Edwardian scene

(these just in terms of tit-show would have earned the film an R-rating if it weren't that the young ladies are just Eskimo girls)

a Hellman type pluviograph and a Bristol gauge recorded rainfall and streamflow for 10 months

her gravid thoughts may well be seeding as if they were microfilm of the sacred books which

she spent most of the time pounding on the typewriter as though beating back the long shadows of her father and older brothers

to pour out my heart to him about my sense of helplessness in the post-devaluation situation

inevitable contradictions in the system, which cannot be reconciled so long as the operation of the system depends on private capital accumulation

imported from the United States and costs 75p a foot. It is described as a plastic-cum-metal that reflects light like crystal.

1975

No one has found a valid goal for history; but everyone has proposed one; and the notion of finality vanishes into a mocking clause of the mind

passive directional low-frequency analyzing and recording equipment will be used

thus the paradox of time travel ceases to exist

soon's you play a little tune on my meat whistle

freshmen, as elsewhere, are subjected to the "pink shower" — the induction into left-wing thought by activist

lifelong compulsive fellators, searching for "fresh meat" at

5 a.m. in a state of maudlin intoxication and undress, without money to defray

the perineal region of the infant shown in plate 7. Note the pseudoclitoris, which is tipped with a tuft of hair

jerked their hydrocephalic heads from side to side above the entrance to a shooting-gallery

and pissed either perfume or medicinal alcohol, distilled by powerful body processes from what they have been, all day long, drinking

there I sat in front of the telly, watching films of gorillas humping other gorillas

the titless and knee-dimpled Annette leading the other Mousketeers into inquiring of the viewers their familiar and rhetorical Why and in singsongy lachrymose unison

stated the fact of the riot and the rock-throwing, but in the overnights and follow-ups one could feel the need for

regions of space to play different roles in contributing to the assembly as a whole functioning as a T.V. set.

1976

Old time carefree train travel is back again. On our rail cruises you'll visit the most exciting places on our continent and

a flat slotted-waveguide antenna, 1,000 meters in diameter, will beam the output to a hybrid

young woman, a theatre dancer and quasi-prostitute, responds to his advances

this prompted Carter to a high, sustained, quiet-shining music for piccolo and violin, disturbed by a restless flickering from marimba

there were 29 wreaths, posies and sprays and specially selected children's hymns were sung at the service

there was widespread doping and he had even taken a drug usually given to horses to help him prolong

prostitution directly from brief careers as topless waitresses, nude models, exotic dancers and body-rub attendants

because being "high" on LSD they felt tempted to leap out of the window

what a pity they did not go to the "Shorter Oxford" where they would have found

varying combinations of Autumn Dusk, Tawny Maize, Adriatic Blue, all attractively designed to set off the cosy glow of a real fire

and sell a variety of moonshine liquors, including a near-lethal combination called ai-ai, which boasts a base of airplane fuel

the girls were Linda Lewis (the current holder of the Miss Leicester title) Anne-Marie Malin (Miss She and Holiday Princess) Dena Patrick (Dairy Princess)

struck the radar nose-dome of a TWA Boeing 707 as it was about to land at Shannon Airport

the re-creation of the plane crash and the depiction of cannibalism in this film may be too intense for sensitive people!

1977

This man is waiting for your pissloads. He has taken 32 pissloads this evening. Free beer to those who piss on him

including Toby, Colt 45, Bass, Black Label, Worthington E, Double Diamond, Youngers, Mackeson, Newcastle Brown, Carlsberg, Prize medal, Jubilee

stands for all the existing drunken men in our real world and in every possible world. He is an open expression (or sign-vehicle)

of neuropharmacology at McGill University where in 1974 he suffered a myocardial infarction. His knowledge was found to be less than professorial and calls to McGill failed to substantiate

most situational feelings are so closely tied to everyday patterns of thought, values, and actions that they appear to be merely the effects of

the sentences underlying these combinations and their predicative counterparts "the drink contains (much) alcohol" and "the smile expresses (much) irony"

since then, the Moon has been a "dead" planetary body, except for continued meteorite cratering, including the Copernicus rayed crater

I have seen the building drift moonlit through geraniums

at the heart of the stainless-steel and glass structure lie two inner courtyards, panelled in striking blond oak and covered by plexidome skylights

where Vincent Price creates a race of post-Frankenstein

adult females, by switching on juvenile signals, re-motivate him from a critical companion into a care-giving pseudo-parent

lesbianism became a valid polito-sexual identity

reaches orgasm as she sees herself splatter her fecal contents over the strangers observing the scene

she touches her children, and they rotate in the oven of her love.

1978

So far we have considered gaps common to all narratives regardless of

a long list of the sources for quotations and paraphrases in the poem. Unfortunately, the more closely we inspect this

penetration of divinity into flesh and the possibility henceforth acquired by it to penetrate into divinity — is called

personhole! ... Personhole? What are you talking about? ... Waah!

some aspects of machine vision such as edge detection, segmentation, and shape representation

change like a rain-dappled pool with his changing musical moods

refracted the sound of voices and laughter and seemed to suspend it in midair

creating terms or names for things by using material from the whole proposition which describe the things' properties

when the ordinary patterns of accepted behaviour are broken, they resort quickly to what may be called quasi-rationalistic explanation

a macho movie actor and a retired newscaster, neither of whom has any pharmacological expertise

would only be able to say "the sun follows the dawn" in a way that might also be

puffed up with abstractitis, love of long words, pleonasm and circumlocution

I did, on request, prescribe phenobarbiturates at night to help her sleep

in addition, may of these nets are lost and continue "ghost fishing" — marine animals keep getting caught in their undegradable plastic fibre for an indefinite period.

1979

The Nixon in my dream may fail to resemble the actual Nixon in crucial ways (lacks

the other side with interrogatories and requests for documents that are repetitious, irrelevant, intrusive and sometimes nonsensical

skin glue can be purchased in either pearls or small chips

recurrent dreams seem often to be statements about unsolved

individuals and groups to project onto the external world a contrived symbolic pattern of paired opposites which embody

the characteristics of the maker, such as the style of the scroll and the shape of the f-holes

a kind of social history, albeit rambling and largely disconnected, of "shit"

but recognizing the unity of things, the profane threads in the holy and the holy in the

esoteric pejoratives, grandiloquisms, and cacophemisms

advising the status seeking partygoer to take up a commanding position in the room

we are all fulfilment men; we all seek the center that will allow the senses to rest

receive letters from the wife of a quietaholic, complaining of her husband, whose only fault is his

foot appears as if it rested on a recumbent animal

the nipples are perspex, suggesting at once the hardness of tumescence and the ice of frigidity.

1980

I was always reminded of pictures, images, in places where images never were, in marble, in the blue net of veins at my wrists

the placket of muscle in the web of the thumb

fingernails bitten down to the quick and stained by nicotine

these structures of organ, organism, and ecosystem belong to a series of analogical integrities that begins with the organelle and

from there it drains into a watertight pit. The small-scale pig keeper may be able to make use of all the slurry produced by allowing it to rot and then using

the Rapture Preparation Crusade in a series of Messages to the People of Britain having visions of a

heat flash and starts fires by setting alight curtain materials, upholstery, clothing — anything inflammable not shaded from the flash

result in mobilisation of large amounts of nutrients both during the fire, and subsequently as a result of stimulated biological mineralisation

indicating that penile erections are related to dream content

he jots down metaphors which then wait for a place in a poem

he describes how after the execution he is anally raped by Uncle Sam himself

started having strange thoughts in the middle of the sex act

the engineer with his screwdriver, rogering iron, piston and pumphandle

lie broken open under the moon, only an icy light thinking inside.

1981

Truth-tellers of all descriptions stood in anxious need of clothing their figures in lineaments

as rare as rocking horse excreta

orchestrated of rapid cutting, sound overlaps, voyeuristic perspective

these texts described arduous ascents through celestial palaces and visions of the Throne-Chariot of the Supreme Being

that dark and sinister hole which went through the middle rig of the ship to the sea underneath

its banks populated with the vermicular strapfeet, the sphinx, the harpy

the hysterical woman and the masturbating child along with entomologized sexological categories such as zoophiles, zooerasts and gynecomasts, typifying

depletion of coke stocks, further failures in the recuperator blast air preheater and failures of condenser refractories resulted in a number of extended furnace outages

demonstrate a reduction in the number of spermatozoa per ejaculate associated with

distracting behaviour of any kind — speaking loudly, shouting in the street, excessive gesticulating, whistling, singing, playing radios

this means that in the dream there is a character who represents Nixon. There may be

understanding of living processes, the very idea that there may be a ghost in the machine amounts to absurdity

clasp your hands behind your back, let your head and back drop down as far as you can

you can start or quit fighting evil at any time, and decide specifically which evils you will fight, on any timeline.

1982

The poet, lacking the impediment of speech with which the rest of us are afflicted

let his mind slip into a new time-dimension. The near future looked good

to preview the performance from the points of view of lighting, sounds, camera angles and sets

looking for the truth about mankind and its creations. He and his team search the garbage dumps of the United States, hoping to start a

theme which is nothing other than the sum, or rather the arrangement of its diverse modulations

constructs his masterwork, a gigantic edifice of old pipes and boilerplate

a cafe-bar-filling station, four-unit motel, trailer, and water tower all huddled on an expanse of dry lakebed mudflats cracked into a crazed jigsaw

of rainbeaten trash, smashed bottles, gutted bedsprings spraying in a flyblown drowse among cinders and slag

which can release delayed-action area-denial mines a well as runway-cratering bomblets

over-temperature shutdown is indicated by illumination of the LED

can arise when blood pressure breaks through one or two layers of the artery wall, or through the entire wall

to write about tradition, memory and anamnesis is to trace subtle processes of storage

a theory with the same signs and theorems and whose axioms form

a magical, fertile, liferestoring stream of words/water/urine.

1983

We are authorized liquidators of consumer products that must be quickly sold at drastic price reductions for reasons such as

an event or series of events in the phylogenetic history of the human species

the defending workers used their mandibles against the intruder

engaged in autoerotic asphyxia in pairs as a means of protection from accidental death

could hear the lack of animation in his voice and see the lack of verve in his face when he watched his own television ads

"I will be the Commissioner for good times for people, plants and animals," he said. "I will be a man for all species"

one day in the laboratory, however, he accidentally tapped on the recording cage while a record was being made from the brain of a cat in slow-wave sleep. Almost immediately a PGO spike

is intentional if it contains or is founded on (recourse to metaphor is difficult to avoid) a thought

of immediate suffering, in which rawness of feeling is untempered by the skills and benefits of art

thousands of encounters and conversations, hundreds of workshops, were so vivid and vital that to put their essence on paper seemed like

the ironic consciousness which has to recover its energy after each failure by reinscribing the failure into the

pub conversation may well transmit information, but what also bulks large in such dialogue is a strong element of

one car going out of control on the rain slicked road at 11.35 pm and it continued over the next few minutes as

a sentence fragment or a run-together sentence.

1984

It seemed to me that I was ravishingly beautiful

was altogether pert, my hair was electrically rectilinear, like a sheet of negative particles

rectangular coordinate robots with a rectangular work envelope have been developed for precision assembly applications

the procedure is said to recurse. When one mental state initiates another, we say that recursion has occurred

reacted almost instantaneously to climatic amelioration and spread rapidly northwards

invaded the grey matter of the spinal cord and the medulla and motor cortex of the brain, with neuronal necrosis, viral destruction and

all manner of guesses and frighteners swarm through a gray matter that's basically angry that the rest of the body's dozing just

before a ray of light can reach the retina it has to pass through the cornea, the aqueous humour, the lens and the vitreous humour

these colours we see by are blind, which is why we must praise them

if a clairovoyant being could have beheld the earth at the moment of the crucifixion he would have seen it beginning to ray forth a light

recursively looping along the line like a sewing machine closing a seam by following the internal directions of the sentence

will protect against ultraviolet rays, and the mousse will moisturize the hair, executives said

officials point to radar maps that trace the departure rates of northbound planes

set their course for the left verge of the Sun's realm.

1985

Set in motion by some accident: there is the texture of the paper, the stains, the hatchings, the tracery of strokes, the diagrams

a way of using the Aztec pictographs to convey Christian ideas such as

the mucous membrane thrown into a series of longitudinal folds termed the rectal columns of Morgagni

the discontinuities in the refractive indices within a leaf determine

the reader as *operating* on the text

an animal's wordlessness takes on the cleansing qualities of space

yups casually unpocketing gold plastic for a $70 plastic palm tree or a $1,500 plasma clock

mothers planning a "pink party" for the occasion of their daughter's first period

giant antennae could be toppling dream material into some profounder pacific state

that charge up the body's electrical impulses so much that overly sedentary viewers explode in their chairs

we have skyhooks and pole stretchers and left-handed monkey wrenches

creams containing stabilised placental cellular extracts

within the head fast catches up with slow by the time slow has gone partway around

dreams the most natural way to obtain a solution.

1986

New terms for marijuana seemed to emerge almost hourly

artexing, pebble-dashing, terylening, gyproc-covering, wall & floor tiling, floor screeding. Free quotations

and cash flow you've always dreamed about. Specialising in donuts, hot and decorated, milkshakes, thickshakes, softserve icecream, 16 flavours of

the complex wiring system connecting all parts of the cortex, suggesting that the gray matter is equipotent in all its parts for any cerebral activity

displays variously grouped granulations, striae, plicae and costae

accumulating memories of childhood in neurotically archivistic notebooks which she exhibits as works of art

prompted former city secretary Charlotte Sharp to break down in tears as she described a lewd mouth gesture Martinez made during a $400 champagne dinner

progressed to catatonia, visual disturbances, disorientation of time and place, short-term memory loss, emotional lability with clouded

out-of-body experience and the glimpsing of a bright portal of light that we call

a solitary, stale pork pie under a perspex dome

a brain floated beneath the extended black plastic snout of a Sony holoptics projector

she began to go to the machine late at night. This way, they could talk without being disturbed

the heroine rounds the curve and sees the House, where she might intercept her future/confront her devils/test

pleasurable activities involving the mouth, including suckling, eating, smoking, kissing, biting, thumb sucking, talking, and oral sex.

1987

People's hopes and sensations must somehow be connected, however haphazardly, like beads on the slenderest of threads

a series of experiments on precognition in

node-negative women from the tissue bank for whom

the ravening of time and the puniness of memory's attempts to withstand it

comprise a wide variety of embouchures (lip positions), singing into the instrument while playing, flutter-tonguing, the use of mutes, stoppers, rubber plungers and

return by subway-mouth to life again, bearing the morning papers, and cross the park where saintlike men, white and absorbed

focus their attention on a deep brain structure

(called "ghosting"), and shunting them round the system to spend a month in a different prison and then

escape from the vermiform parent into the host urine and then into the sea

bone cement is placed in the medullary cavity, the fractures reduced and held together until the cement hardens

each spectator was given a "ghost-viewer", an obscure twist on 3-D glasses

the coconut-like sound of their heads colliding secretly delighted the bird

by taking an overdetermined text (a cartoon, a bestseller) and subjecting it to a systematic misreading. This reinscription

requires the reader to yield patiently to its structural development, as a correlative to the principle of humility articulated by the sentence.

1988

The female breast was a high-intensity area for semiotic activity, and every dressmaker knew

the continuous activity of selecting, omitting and organizing the details of reality so that we experience the world as

a psychomimetic version of their relation to the TV image. They seem to be trying to read by proprioception and exploratory touch. The printed page, however

exhibits the labour of writing, with all the first lines, the crossed-out sentences, whited-out lines with fragments of letters showing though

in a quiet setting the toy, shaped like a river rock, emits the gentle river sounds of the Shimanto River in Shikoku

the poet's reason for not writing in a particular style or on a particular subject

to enumerate is to make conceivable, therefore fungible, therefore easily obliterated

night, unstratified space, peaceful or desolate landscapes, death, silence and emptiness

put me into a bed with a ghostwoman; she painted blood on her lips and her breath smelt of

sheets soaked with perspirations, hair saturated with fetor, body limp with exhaustion

time kaleidoscopes. The past is refracted back and forth, becomes the present, is highlighted by it, is illuminated by it, is replaced by it

I seem to be drifting into a phantasmagoria of analogies or substitutions

I refrain from synthesizing these quotations from various knowledges into a cultural totality

questions of a subterranean dialectic of consequences never arose.

1989

A century of deflected philosophical investigation was coming to an end, and artists were

forced to enter into a dialogue or debate with their predecessors, recycling bits and pieces of earlier texts

towards times later than an arbitrary instant t, and does not imply a commitment to the theory of time which asserts the physical reality of "past", "present" and

they raise the middle and forefingers of both hands, momentarily forming twitchy bunny ears — air quotes

their waking thoughts, & occasionally their dreams are filled with minor guilts

indulged in "bad painting" with sardonic parody, hallucinatory eclecticism and incisive political wit

these postfeeding psychic effects originate to some extent in the gastrointestinal tract

yet this did not stop him thinking. He was given the Ravens Matrices as an intelligence test

stimuli were presented in the centre of a Joyce Electronics raster display via a Cambridge Electronics Design interface system

cerebral irritability, shock, deteriorating feeding skills, a bulging fontanelle with a rapidly expanding head

variations in type, including capital letters and varying sizes of print to indicate the relative loudness of the utterance

the line of words felt for cracks in the firmament

unreeled around him in his childhood like the spokes of a milky galaxy

exfoliating, detail upon detail, like a crystal compulsively elaborating its own structure.

1990

A totally academicized poet produces an autobiographical poem which is a collage of all Western Literature

its high point is a passage that underlines his ability in the delicate terrain of dream-poetry

stimuli consisted of 150 concrete picturable noun exemplars, plus 30 miscellaneous objects

these shards he collected also share, at least implicitly, a solicitude for the small and the vulnerable

this detonates a chain of events that unhinges the structure of his family

is information stored through time

Time dependent data, Event calculus, Persistence through time — the Frame Problem, Temporal query language, Temporal transactions

opens us to ambitious synthetic visions, the elaborate ray tracing and fractal generation of scenes that never actually existed, from skyscrapers to still-life poses of luscious

branches and leaves moulded from phenolic foam to look like the crown of a palm tree

two pointers then appear. One is a crosshair for typing over the document, the other is a pencil that allows you to

position the eyes so that the image of a certain target or element of the visual scene falls

from a new type of picture-in-picture television set. While offering the viewer a menu of images from eight different channels at once, it creates ironic

themes, which often elliptically relate to the apparent context, and sometimes even

secures the regularity of musical sounds and the people spontaneously agree in harmony and compliance.

1991

Consider how x-rays, CAT scans, and radio telescopes have altered human perception and

perceive the pulsation of time

specify which ways of filling out the space around the perceiver are consistent with the veridicality of the experience

reproduce buck and doe grunts, bleats and lost-contact calls, breeding bleats and "mews" of fawns

avoid processed meat products

get together an impressive if somewhat grey-templed team of professors emeriti to design, execute and analyse a definitive study

watch eclipses, transits, occultations

pay homage to the symbol of isolation, the satellite dish

scan through a timeline of collaged family photographs from 1890 to the present

monitor patients for neurological changes

finish with the past in the sense of removing its power to hurt us and to stunt our growth as human beings

distrust the wavering ticktockishness of the shrinking and of the enlargement of the self

use a flat latex device held over the vagina

put commodities of all kinds into narrativity, make them labile sexual encounters.

1992

Over a lunch of arugula and sun-dried tomato salad with Paramount executives, a ray-banned Gorbachev negotiates a three-picture deal, with a high back-end

the writer engages rather in a scriptorial operation that could be described as

reading biology texts as steamy poetry, stock market listings as epic

transported in a purpose-built complex back through time. There will be at least 12 visitor interaction experiences and a themed

Nigeria possessed some 20m "ghosts": nonexistent people who have registered to vote

the Banking Information Service claims phantom withdrawals are impossible and complaints are the result of fraud by

born again believers, who number about 28 million in the US, and will be raptured into pure spirit

somewhere above it all, this new disembodied mind could systematically and relentlessly decipher the scientific laws that would allow us

while dancing, to eventually select a smooth area on the ground, where he releases and attaches a package of sperm

a tie deftly covers up the button placket running down the front of your shirt, allowing you to present a neat and cohesive experience

for time travel. The form echoes Deco, but the canted angles and curved arms sweep you comfortably into the future

windows depicting the content of each input sequence displayed in the form of time lines running across the screen

provide you with a world of capabilities including variational design drafting, raster editing, redlining

therefore, the world of objects is essentially made of speech.

P.O.V. thru night vision glasses of claw on fence wires

artificially inducing sexual receptivity, they inseminated the animal
with sperm flown by airfreight

recursive thickets of code blocking her memory stood out against the
elegant

cases in which female species do have storage crypts where sperm
survival is

studied by white-coated doctors looking for signs of sexual deviancy,
lack of racial awareness, and ideological doubt

just as a text decontextualizes itself from its conditions of production
by surviving as a material trace through time, so

as dessicated motes with all systems switched off, these endobacterial
spores travel through time in search of

virtual subculture peopled by chaos junkies, quasi-mutant pseudo-
satanists, dead people of cyberspace

a man whose forehead suggested he had just had a cheap craniotomy
and his

library of depictions of space is far richer than that: across the globe
and through time, artists have invented a wealth of

virtuoso muscular performance aimed at sucking vaginal contents,
sperm included, towards

the railroad which caused the death of his family by tampering with
the computer system so that two supertrains

have been "ghosted" (white eggshell paint wiped on and off to leave
streaks in the grain) to complement the

journey into what she calls the "parallel universes" inhabited by the
antagonists in the false memory controversy.

1994

As chemical shadows flit through the mind, scientists can spy on

the cycle of fear that they were victimized by satanists as children

yet fathers who have been paying maintenance in the past are still
being confronted with

a powerful information molecule able to tell surrounding cells

the initiatory ordeals of their quest — night-sea journeys,
swordbridges, labyrinths, lethal riddles, category transcensions

expressions of interest from companies wishing to be included in the
market testing of the following elements of its debt recovery services:
— monies due as the result of the breakdown of spousal maintenance

called a multiverse. Each contains its own copy of the neutron whose
decay we wish to observe

one in which fact, fantasy and suggestion become interchangeable and
accepted with equal ease as

coupled in some unexplained way and can transmit their motion to all
lower concentric spheres

every time I stop typing, the screen saver kicks in and a small
bitmapped image of Starfleet's patron saint of logic materializes on my
monitor

his records and live performances generate phase-shifted universes of
delayed, controlled and manipulated sounds

to fall pregnant as soon as possible, she keeps dragging him off to the
stockroom for a quickie! But he wouldn't be so chuffed if he knew the
reason behind Bev's scheming

red pixels shift as the computer frames the image forward through time

now and then the flatlines gave a spooky twitch, as if something
continued to struggle inside the boy, some destroyed fragment of his
soul.

1995

The following report introduces the hardware design of a neuro-
computer aligned to simulate large neural nets consisting of

ideas propagating across populations and through time

open easily at the touch of a hand, close and latch automatically after
each manual use

a *sous conversation*, a ghost-text, as in the many layers, literal and
metaphorical, of

an object that has been hidden. The infant does not have an enduring
mental representation of

a set of wooden boxes, called coffins, used for meteor observing

that register the momentary glow produced when a cosmic ray
generates a shower of particles on a moonless night

he notes a hotel's strange bed, whose recurrent dream we are

project our imagination into space and time through the virtuality of
the material as a free and compassionate agent searching for

in vitro cultures of honesty for the first time and subjecting them to a
process called protoplast fusion

the companies have signed undertakings to stop the conduct,
reimburse the consumers and establish a compliance program to
ensure

an almighty crunch through the two crusts of bread, followed by a
wadge of mayo and smattering of tommy sauce to take away the hard
impact of

a powerful chain of chemical reactions. Called the glutamate cascade,
it rains terrible destruction down on brain cells

from this day onwards, he was rainbow sexuality, hard glamour and
infernal vocals.

Consciousness is software, a program runnable on any hardware as intricate as human

images that are dancing from modem to modem in the evening or the exact repetition of words from previous texts in the work of

the ghost of Shakespeare in a white coat, sometimes as bartender, sometimes as psychiatrist

the digital-effects artist used these facial uses to animate Kennedy's image and sync his mouth movements with the scripted dialogue

never dreamed they were raising their own executioners

overwhelm my project with easy erudition and inhibit my will to

a continuous text ceaselessly being written, revised, expanded and edited, while

the many rhythms expressed by living things in the real world are

disembodied voices that live in the cockpit from which they speak to us soothingly

at the Nixon Centre for Peace and Freedom, speakers pointed out that the phenomenon of mass terrorism is spreading

the portion of the interpreter that loads machine-specific library routines from its runtime library was flawed

injected stuff from the brains of mad cows into the skulls of macaque monkeys, and sent them mad too

at a gathering a few days later the plagiariser was savagely attacked and almost killed

with murals of flowers, with New Age symbols and icons, with dragons and dancers and with theatre and play.

1997

The voices of many people have mingled with my own to create this

perception of the complex network of relationships, links and affinities between old texts and new

shadowy, even rhetorical presences who play no part in the discursive economy of the text

charge commercial appropriation of her voice, which she says was remixed and added to a song called "Fuck 'Em"

he liked using a condom because it had a sleek metallic shimmer, like his favourite weapons system, the Honest John

has a wonderful job, a loving husband, and two adorable children

long wigs and cherubic faces make them look like girls, but

you'll be involved in maintaining and repairing the electrical generation and distribution systems and the general systems

these letters, accusing well-known local men of adultery, fornication and incest, caused an enormous amount of

cognitive dissonance by focussing on the benefits of documentation procedures

results from the death of nerve cells in the part of the brain that generates dopamine, a chemical messenger that

spray-painted the American Institute of Certified Public Accountants logo over some of the kids' graffiti

by borrowing tactics from the tabloid science writer who sees connections, unities, and paradoxes in most things

and the strangeness of a universe which has produced creatures like ourselves.

1998

Several models of speech/language production have been proposed that incorporate multiple levels of processing

in each case, the speaker starts to produce a literal version of something, but then does a self-repair which substitutes a figurative description

thus, the verb in the phrase *open the door very slowly* licenses *door* and

the criteria for deciding where to locate a new MacDonald's will come to resemble the criteria for making several of the choices one makes in writing a poem

displays a coherence of its own, which is secured by lexical chains and simple cohesive devices

the person who feels impressed at what the ground floor contains cannot be made an explicit participant with this wording of the process

can communicate globally and search remote library catalogues without leaving the comfort of his own study

moves away from traditional UK approaches, based on the rapid transfer of roof and paved surface runoff to

build up in layers that are kilometres thick, forming abyssal plains as smooth as the

ghostly presence of all the books that went before and left no mark on the world

after observing the story with a child, a second experimenter covered her eyes

but is also a specific way of using (reading/writing) a poem: i.e., assembling words or phrases from pre-exisiting poems that

found their way into the London Underground 100 years ago are evolving into a new species with a taste for

marginalized groups. Just as they are "entering history" the power and truth value of historical accounts are rendered unstable.

1999

The very act of writing a sonnet establishes this act as a signifier

but the twentieth century, he concluded, is best expressed via its own media

a society likened to a human brain, with the individuals who form it functioning as so many

search engines and data mining tools that decide by themselves how information should be structured

each character also seems motivated by an urgent but futile private agenda. A woman tries, lovingly, to feed crumbs to an origami duck

college professors start to fight back with their own cyberspace tactics

infect thousands of computers and overload e-mail systems worldwide

and thousands of sources will appear in a matter of

a clock-defying world where financial markets run continuously and news channels promise never-ending

giving. For every visitor who clicks the button, a hungry person in the world gets a meal

I flew over the site once. It was dark and it looked just like Bristol. I couldn't believe

that the Government was preparing for a knowledge economy in the new

years in a fast-moving montage of memorable moments with music and scrolling newsbites

throughout the century's poetry and all highlight the importance of thinking about literature as texts weaved by and weaving the historical discourses that surround.

Sources

(Dates in brackets refer to the republication, when it was not possible to consult the original edition.)

1900 E Holmes *What Is Poetry?* 5; A Buck *Handbk. Medical Science* (rev ed) I. 647; W Dorland *Medical Dict.* 50/1; J Joyce in *Century Mag.* Jan. 386/1; M Twain *Man That Corrupted Hadleyburg* 135; *Congressional Records* 5 Feb. 1521/2; G Patten *Rockspur Nine* 149; F Jackson *Hist. Hand-Made Lace* 189; *Fortnightly Rev.* Apr. 578; E Brodhead *Eternal Feminine* 765 ; L Baum *Wonderful World Oz* 21; L Woolf 9 Apr. *Letters Leonard Woolf* (1989) 15; J Jastrow *Fact & Fable in Psychol.* 57; R Fry in *Monthly Rev.* Dec. 152

1901 W Scawen Blunt 23 Jan. *My Diaries* (1919) II 2; C Cox *Visits to Jesus & Mary* 130; F Norris *Octopus* (1964) 151; E Titchener *Exper. Psychol* I 338; *Jrnl. Exper. Med* VI 69; R Kipling *Kim* 197; *Daily Chron.* 17 Aug. 8/4; H Wells *First Men in Moon* 116; G Ade *40 Mod. Fables* 70; G Dickinson *Letters from John Chinaman* 13; *Chambers's Jrnl.* Nov. 717/1; M Foster *Lectures on Hist. Physiol.* 175; *Daily Chron.* 23 Sept. 3/4; *Munsey's Mag.* XXIV 875/2

1902 G Lorimer *Letters Merchant* 214; *Encycl. Brit.* XXXI 680/1; *Westminster Gaz.* 3 Aug. 4/2; A Waite *Doctrine & Lit. Kabalah* I 27; *Lancet* 1902 quoted *ibid* 3 Sept. 1977 505/2; E Banks *Autobiog. Newspaper Girl* 122; *Daily Chron.* 11 July 5/1; A McFaul *Ike Glidden* 257; W James *Varieties Relig. Experience* 135; W Scawen Blunt *My Diaries* (1919) II 17; H Wilson *Spenders* 429; *Daily Chron.* 7 Nov. 4/2; Lord Avebury *Scenery of England* 477; R Grey *Myself When Young* 11

1903 H. Munsterburg *Harvard Psychol. Stud.* I. 644; R Fry 6 Mar. in *Letters* (1972) 204; H James *Ambassadors* (1909) II 4; *Encycl. Americana* VIII s.v. 'harmonists'; W Savage in *Athletics & Outdoor Sports for Women* 48; H Keller *Story of My Life* I 50; *Sun* (NY) 23 Nov. 12; A Lang *Valet's Tragedy* 205; J Matthews *Mass & Folklore* 63; A McNeill *Egregious English* 151; W Spinks *House Drainage Manual* (2nd Ed) 7; B Lees 'Preface' *Hist. in Biography* III v; *New Eng. Dict. on Hist. Principles* VI (preface); *Electrical World & Engineering* 26 Dec. 1034

1904 *NY Evening Post* 2 Jan. 3/1; W James *Essays in Radical Empiricism* 77; S Bushell *Chinese Art* 139; *Popular Science Monthly* Jan.195; *Sci. Amer.* 27 Feb. 23545; *Blackwoods Mag.* Apr. 588/1; F Moore *Original Woman* xii; 'Number 1500' *Life in Sing-Sing* 260; *Collier's Mag.* 7 May 20/3 (advt); M Twain *Diaries of Adam & Eve* 7; V Lean *Collectanea* 19; R Whitman *Orthopedic Surgery* (ed. 2) 573; *Nature* 19 May 50/1; *Biometrika* III 99

1905 W Brann *Brann the Iconoclast* X 163; A White *Autobiog.* 499; E Benson *Image in Sand* ix; M Hamilton *Kingdoms Curious* 68; F Burnett *Dawn of Tomorrow* 19; J Shirazi tr. M Gorky *Creatures That Once Were Men* 1; H Clothrop 'The Only Woman in Town' in *Twilight Stories* (no page ref.); Baroness Orczy *Scarlet Pimpernel* chap. 28 (no page ref.); G MacDonald *Phantastes: A Faerie Romance for Men & Women* 44; I Burnett *Little Princess* 176; T Green's *Pathol.* (ed. 10) 11; E Wharton *House of Mirth* (1993) 7; *Westminster Gaz.* 4 May 12/1; G Tarde 'Underground Man' in G Negley ed. *Quest for Utopia* (1952) 193-4

1906 F Maitland 1 May in *Letters* (1965) 372; C Wright *Battles of Labour* 131; *Washington Post* 28 May 3; *Daily Chron.* 30 June 9/1; *Month* July 66; J Galsworthy *Man of Property* 187; E Dyson *Fact'ry 'Ands* 51; O Henry *Four Million* (1916) 131; H Ellis *Studies in Psychol. Sex* V 71; C Sherrington *Integrative Action Nervous System* 330; C Pierce *Coll.*

Papers IV (1933) II 438; *Daily Chron.* 14 Nov. 3/4; *Practitioner* Nov. 712; *Mod. Lang. Notes* XXI 184/1.

1907 *Jrnl. Philos., Psychol. & Sci. Methods* 200; *Collier's* 26 Jan. 14/1; J Illingworth *Doctrine of the Trinity* 10; *Daily Chron.* 25 Feb. 3/2; *St Nicholas* May 595/2; *Macmillan Mag.* Feb. 319; A Dieffendorf *Clin. Psychiatry* (ed. 2) 68; *Daily Chron.* 3 Sept. 7/5; S Joyce diary in R Ellman *James Joyce* (1983) 265; J Synge *Playboy of Western World* in *Coll. Wks.* (1910) II 54-5; 7 Edward VII cap.53 in C Knight, ed. *Public Health Acts* (1913); *Army & Navy Stores Catalogue* 1044/1; *Westminster Gaz.* 12 Dec. 9/4; *Daily Chron.* 17 Dec. 4/6

1908 H Fisher 'A Mutt' in B Blackbeard & M Williams eds. *Smithsonian Coll. Newspaper Comics* (1977) 58; F Francis & J Fortescue-Brickdale *Chem. Basis Pharmacol.* 83; *Practitioner* Jan, 12; *Daily Chron.* 8 Apr. 3/6; G Lorimer J *Spurlock* 2; *Sears Roebuck Catalogue* 241/5; E Wharton 17 May in R & N Lewis *Letters Edith Wharton* (1988) 145; *Daily Chron.* 18 May 3/5; *Westminster Gaz.* 26 May 6/3; H Bradly 'Preface to Letter M' *New Eng. Dict.* VI; G Chesterton *All Things Considered* 195; V Asquith 19 Oct. in M Bonham Carter & M Pottle eds. *Diaries & Letters Violet Bonham Carter* (1997) 166; E Benson *Climber* 140; G Saintsbury *Cambridge Hist. Eng. Lit.* II. 191

1909 C Saleeby *Parenthood & Race Culture* 206; *Daily Chron.* 19 Feb. 6/5; E Temple Thurston *City of Beautiful Nonsense* 172; S White *Rules of Game* I 102; C Saleeby *Alcohol & Infancy* 9; H James *Ambassadors* (1909 ed.) preface; R Wason *Happy Hawkins* 277; F Warner *Our Invisible Supply, How to Obtain* 41; Q Ewing *Heart of Race Problem* 394; G Woodhead *Alcohol & Disease, an Address* 9; W Blunt 15 Mar. in *My Diaries* II 244; *Granta* 11 June in J Philip et al *Best Of Granta* (1967) 42; A Burton *Memories of Childhood's Slavery Days* (1988) 6; *Westminster Gaz.* 19 Apr. 5/4

1910 A Perry *Problems of Elementary School* 201; *Daily Chron.* 15 Jan. 9/1; *Encycl. Brit.* Vol I s.v. acne; *Westminster Gaz.* 10 Feb. 5/1; S Bushell *Chinese Art* II 38; *Practitioner* Apr. 520; *Brixton Free Press* 21 Sept. 'Theatre Gossip'; R Kipling *Diversity of Creatures* 313; W Locke *Simon the Jester* 77; *Blackwoods Mag.* 82/1; *Los Angeles Times* Jan. 10 1/6; H Richardson *Getting of Wisdom* (1982) xv. 127; R Casement diary (presumed) 18 Oct. in *London Rev. Bks.* 2 Oct. 1997 26/4; R Brooke 22 Dec. in *Letters* (1968) 327

1911 *Proc. Musical Association* 121; A Godley *Casual Ward* 64; *Jrnl. Political Econ.* 19 287; J Glover *Jimmy Glover — His Book* 234; H. Gross *Criminal Psychol.* (unpaginated); H & G Fowler Preface to *Concise Oxford Dict.* v; C Peel *How to Keep House* 40; *Confessions of a Dancing Girl by Herself* 65; J Thomson *Biol. of Seasons* 193; C Mercier *Conduct & Its Disorders* 111; P Schidrowitz *Rubber* 196; *Cosmopolitan* Jan. 231; J Anderson *Grammar of Case* 140; J Conrad 20 Oct. in E Garnett ed. *Letters* (1956) 234

1912 A Keith *Human Body* 116; F Talbot *Motor-Cars* 35; C Mackenzie *Carnival* 347; A Lewis *Apaches of N.Y.* 41; E Porter *Miss Billy's Decision* 16; J Galsworthy *Inn of Tranquility* 48; J Stephens *Charwoman's Daughter* 46; A Pendleton *Seagoing Experiences of One Heck* Haskins 34; *Medical Annual* 458; A Brill tr. S Freud *Sel. Papers Hysteria* (ed. 2) 210; J Conrad *'Twixt Land & Sea* 60; L Woolf 29 Apr. *Letters* (1989) 174; T Dreiser *Financier* (1967) 312; A Way tr. *Euripides* IV 205

1913 E Bentley *Trent's Last Case* (1995) 5; E Pound 'Serious Artist' in *Literary Essays* (1960); D Barnes in A Berry ed. *New York* (1989) 124; *Maclean's Mag.* Feb.163/1; *Saturday Evening Post* 22 Feb. 24/1; *Jrnl. Philos. & Psychol.* X 270; N Farquhar *Crown of Hinduism* 237; W Bateson tr. G Mendel *Principles Heredity* 71; A Brill tr. S Freud *Interpretation of Dreams* 281; D Lawrence 'Coldness in Love' *Love Poems & Others* 11; D

Barnes in A Berry ibid. 22; E Jones *Papers in Psycho-anal.* 26; M Dana *Within the Law* 174; G Le Bon *Psychol. of Revolution* 296/7

1914 *Women & Other Enigmas* 6; F Bradley *Essays on Truth & Reality* 460; E Pound 'Prose tradition in Verse' *Literary Essays* (1960) 377; W Handy 'St Louis Blues' (song); D Lawrence *Prussian Officer* 12; L Wittgenstein 'Notes Dictated to G Moore in Norway April 1914', in *Notebks. 1914-18* (1979); J Jeans *Report on Radiation & Quantum Theory* 2; C Broad *Perception, Physics, & Reality* 196; J Morley resignation letter to Asquith, 3 Aug., in W Arnstein ed. *Past Speaks* II (1993) 320; J Hastings *Encycl. Religion & Ethics* VII 148/2; Sir E Grey statement to House of Commons 3 Aug. in Arnstein ibid. 309; E Burroughs *Tarzan of Apes* 36; *Glasgow News* 22 Dec. 4; J Joyce *Dubliners* (1974) 216

1915 *Proc. Soc. Antiquaries* XXVII 149; W Cather *Song of Lark* 48; W Stevens 'Blanche McCarthy' in *Palm at End of Mind* (1971) 58; *Daily Mirror* 23 Feb. 4/1; J Palmer *George Bernard Shaw: Harlequin or Patriot?* 777; C Jain *Key of Knowledge* 666; W Owen Apr. *Letters* (1967) 331; C Payne tr. O Pfister *Psycho-analytic Method* 336; A MacLeish 30 July in *Letters* (1983) 16; G Crice *Origin & Nature Emotions* 175; R Brooke 'Fragments written during voyage to Gallipoli' in *Poetical Wks.* (1970) 203; W Osler letter 29 July in H Cushing *Life* (1925); B Bower *Jean of Lazy A* 177-8; E Wharton *Coming Home* 702

1916 A Quiller-Couch *Art of Writing* 91; E Slawson letter 27 Feb. in T Thompson ed. *Dear Girl, Diaries & Letters Two Working Women* (1987) 294; J Chromatin Brown *Dies Heroica* (1918) 93; R Slate diary 13 Mar. in T Thompson ibid. 296; C Ward-Jackson *Airman's Songbk.* (1945); B Russell *Principles Social Reconstruction* 1 (1920); A Pollitzer in C Giboire *Complete Correspondence G O'Keeffe & A Pollitzer* (1990) 162; M Ward *England's Effort: Letters to Amer. Friend* in W Arnstein ed. *Past Speaks* (1993) II 328/2; J Lewis *Old Glass* 62; J Joyce *Portrait of Artist* 85; *Yorkshire Post* 21 July 5/5; R Frost 'Birches' *Mountain Interval*; D Barnes in A Berry *New York* (1989) 246; A MacLeish 11 Nov. in R Winnick ed. *Letters A MacLeish* (1983) 30

1917 Letter 30 April in *Jrnl. Negro Hist.* (1919) 414; H James *Ivory Tower* (1917) notes 287; J Galsworthy *Beyond* (1929) 365; *Manchester Guardian* 16 Mar. 5/1; *Nat. Rev.* Aug. 637; W Locke *Red Planet* xii; D Lawrence 'In the Dark' in *Look! We have Come Through* 43; J Powys 'To Isadora Duncan' *Mandragora* 71; *Literary Digest* 25 Aug. 28/1; E Wallace *Just Men of Cordova* x 169; *Quarterly Rev.* Autumn 35; *Mod. Philol.* XV 450; *Proc. Aristotelian Soc.* 17 431; A Waugh *Loom of Youth* 124

1918 *Observer* 10 Feb. 7/1; A Waley 170 *Chinese Poems* 117; E Pound *Andreas Divus* (1968) 262; S Sassoon 22 Feb. in *Diaries 1915-18*; E Sitwell *Clown's Houses* 8; B Tarkington *Magnificent Ambersons* 435; L Ruggles *Navy Explained* 102; A Huxley 20 May *Letters* (1969) 151; W Cather *My Antonia* 771; *Electricity* 6 Sept. 477/1; H Seymour *Reproduction of Sound* 254; R Bourne 'Earnest' in *Hist. of Literary Radical* (1956) 106; J Conrad 22 Dec. *Letters* (1956) 259; W Owen *Poems* (1931) 69

1919 E O'Neill *Moon of Caribbees* 32; *Psychoanal. Rev.* VI 159; *Outing* Mar. 326/1 (advt.); W Lewis in *Essays on Art, Lit. & Soc.* (1989) 55; J Reed *10 Days That Shook the World* (1926) 268; *Detective Story Mag.* XXVIII 6; E Greenly *Geol. Anglesey* I 193; *Mind* XXVIII 318; J Conrad *Arrow of Gold* 5; M Bradby *Psycho-anal.* 34; *Guardian* (Manchester) 21 Oct. 3/1; *Photoplay* Nov. 72, in *Film Index* (1941); *Proc. Royal Soc.* IVC 355; H Mencken *Amer. Lang.* 305

1920 T Eliot *Sacred Wood* 2; *NY Times* 26 June 8/4; A Eddington *Space, Time & Gravitation* 186; *Glasgow Herald* 21 July 8; P Wodehouse *Coming of Bill* 25; *Amer. Woman* Aug. 8/2;

Amer. Jrnl. Physiol. LII 209; N Bessaraboff tr. P Ouspensky *Tertium Organum* 92; Sir A Geddes to Earl Curzon 18 Oct. in *British Documents on Foreign Affairs* Part 2 Series C vol I (1986) 46; G Robey *After Dinner Stories* 9; *Jewish Peril: Protocols of the Learned Elders of Zion* 14; *Amer. Econ. Rev.* X 157; W Walsh *Psychol. Dreams* 189; E Watkin in C Hess *God & Supernatural* 141

1921 R Paine *Comrades of Rolling Ocean* 73; D Lawrence *Women in Love* (1960) 496; M Allen in B Williams *O Henry Prize Stories 1921* (1922); L Strachey *Queen Victoria* (1958) 258; C Blayre *Purple Sapphire* 32; S Sassoon 8 Jan. *Diaries 1920-22*; E Shackleton *South* (cheap edition) preface xiii; *Amer. Woman* Jan. 3/3; E Kempf *Psychopathol.* 326; *Blackwoods Mag.* Apr. 535/2; J Hastings *Encycl. Religion & Ethics* XII 323/2; *Spectator* Apr. 16 480/2; *Times* 29 June 10/6; *Flight* XIII 502/1

1922 H Crane 18 June *Letters* (1965) 92; W Lewis in *Essays on Art, Lit. & Soc.* (1989) 74; S Redgrove *Alchemy Ancient & Mod.* 63; F Harris *My Life & Loves* (1994) 13; C Ainsworth Mitchell *Documents & Their Sci. Evaluation* 47; S Lewis *Babbit* (1961) 82; *Pract. Value Sci. Study Juvenile Delinquents* 8; *Blackwoods Mag.* May 632/3; S Lewis *Babbitt* 123; J Riviere tr. S Freud *Introductory Lectures Psycho-anal.* 264; *TLS* 16/11; E Cummings *Enormous Room* (1971) 55; T O'Rahilly *Misc. Irish Proverbs* 76; *People's Home Jrnl.* July 21/1

1923 P Selver tr. K Capek *R.U.R.* 6; J Hopper in B Williams *O. Henry Prize Stories 1923* (1924) 92; H Belloc 'Homage' *Coll. Verses* (1958) 69; E & C Paul tr. S Freud *Young Girl's Diary* 108; J Ottley *Records Ancient Family* 137; H Mencken *Prejudices* 3rd Series 10; D Lawrence *Fantasia of Unconscious* 145; *Daily Mail* 5 Feb. 7; E Marchant *Radio Telegr. & Teleph.* 34; H Wells *Men Like Gods* 13; C Broad *Sci. Thought* 348; *Nat. Geographic* Apr. 364/2; *Daily Mail* 7 May 7; *Glasgow Herald* 24 Oct. 9

1924 D Marquis *Words & Thoughts* 5; R Mottram *Spanish Farm* (1952) 144; R Ogden tr. K Koffka *Growth of Mind* 118; J Edwards in P Oliver *Screening Blues* (1968) 64; *Dialect Notes* V 265; I Irwin in B Williams *O Henry Prize Stories 1924* (1925) 21; J Riviere et al tr. S Freud *Coll. Papers* I. 90; E Waugh 9 July in *Diaries* (1976) 168; *Amer. Mercury* Sept. 74/2; A Allmond & H Ellingham *Principles Applied Electrochemistry* (ed. 2) 456; W Selbie *Psychol. Religion* 269; *Amer. Mercury* Dec. 5 (advt); E Meagher *Masturbation & Reputed Sequelae* 17; T Wright *Romance Lace Pillow* 80

1925 A Huxley *Those Barren Leaves* (1982) 80; C Fox *Educational Psychol.* 294; C Gahan *Furniture Beetles* 5; I Richards *Science & Poetry* 11; *Internat. Jrnl. Psycho-anal.* VI 419; *Today's Housewife* Feb. 32/1; R Kingston in E Norton *Fight for Everest 1924* 350; *Amer. Mercury* 301/1; F Fitzgerald *Great Gatsby* (1974) 59; H Laski *Grammar of Politics* 86; *Glasgow Herald* 18 Apr. 4; *Internat. Studio* May 495; *O Henry Prize Stories 1925* (1926) 121; V Woolf *Mrs Dalloway* (1942) 73

1926 J Huxley *Essays Popular Science* 5; J Walsh *Photometry* 315; W McDougall *Outline Abnormal Psychol.* 133; E Bowen 'Visitor' *Coll. Stories* (1980) 126; H Morton *Spell of London* 74; A Conan Doyle *Hist. Spiritualism* l 114; *People's Home Jrnl.* Feb. 9/3; W Locke *Old Bridge* 119; *Amer. Mercury* Apr. 494/1; C Van Vechten *Nigger Heaven* 285; *Contemp. Rev.* Aug. 191; G Maines *Wise-crack Dict.* 11; *Travel* Nov. 32/1; D Byrne *Brother Saul* 62.

1927 A Conan Doyle *Case-bk. Sherlock Holmes* 215; A Eddington *Stars & Atoms* 68; E Bowen *Hotel* (1950) 118; *Amer. Mercury* Feb. 195/1; *Sunday Express* 1 May 16; M Stopes *Kagekiyo* 55; *Punch* 27 July 85/3; V Woolf *To The Lighthouse* (1977) 60; *Observer* 14 Aug.

18/1; F Balfour-Browne *Insects* 59; *Glasgow Herald* 22 Oct. 4; *Amer. Pol. Sci. Rev.* XXI 5; A Melchett *Industry & Politics* 211; E Forster *Aspects Novel* 107

1928 *Oxford Poetry* 4; J Buchan *Runagates Club* 305; *Broadcaster* in S Briggs *These Radio Times* (1981) 216/1; M Webb *House in Dormer Forest* 191; *Daily Tel.* 7 Feb. 5/2; *Times* 22 Mar. 1/3; A Kocourek *Jural Relations* (ed 2) 438; C Gamble *Story North Sea Air Station* 232; *Literary Digest* 16 June 9; *Publisher's Weekly* 16 June 2455; *Sunday Express* 24 June 8/3; *Scholartis Press Catalogue* July; Graffito Yosemite National Park July 1928 in A Read *Classic Amer. Graffiti* 54; *Daily* Tel. 28 Aug. 7/5

1929 *Amer. Mercury* Jan. 60/2; J Priestley *Good Companions* 300; G Mitchell *Mystery of Butcher's Shop* 8; M De La Roche *Whiteoaks* 138; R & H Lynd *Middletown* 390; *Oxford Poetry* 2; T Wolfe *Look Homeward, Angel* (1958) 287; P Gibbs *Hidden City* 50; *Programme Communist International* 1; *Encycl. Brit.* XI 747/2; W Miller *To You I Tell It* 214; *Revolutionary Movement in Colonies* 17; C Aiken *Sel. Poems* 48; W Collinson *Spoken Eng.* 82

1930 *G. K.'s Weekly* 26 July 316/2; A Symons *Confessions a Study in Pathol.* 3; J Dos Passos *42nd Parallel* 65; E Sitwell *Alexander Pope* (1948) 13; T Eliot *Ash Wednesday* 11; A Herbert *Water Gipsies* 259; D Lawrence in *Phoenix* II (1968) 45; W Empson *Seven Types Ambiguity* 301; J Jeans *Universe around Us* (ed.2) 329; W Auden *Poems* 16; *TLS* 28 Aug. 683/1; M Connelly *Green Pastures* in *Six Plays* 83; *Electronics* Sept. 269/3; L Wittgenstein in D Lee ed. *Wittgenstein's Lectures 1930-32* (1980) 25/26

1931 R Goodland *Bibliog. Sex Rites* 722; A Dilley *Oriental Rugs & Carpets* 209; L Lewin *Phantastica Narcotic & Stimulating Drugs* 31; *Bull. Seismol. Soc. Amer.* XXI 283; T Eliot 'Triumphal March' *Coll. Poems* (1970) 140; *Advertiser* (Adelaide) 7 Oct.10; E Bowen *Friends & Relations* 98; G Stern *Meaning & Change of Meaning* 290; F Grove *Apologia Pro Vita et Opere Sua* in G Lynch & D Rampton eds. *Canad. Essay* (1991) 54; *Notes & Queries* CLX 110/1; J Cannan *High Table* 161; *Good Housekeeping* Dec. 132/2; G Freeman *Misc. of Frauds & Defalcations* 19; *TLS* 24 Dec. 1036/4

1932 H Jackson *Fear of Books* 25; E Cummings 'Introduction' *Enormous Room* (1971) 7; *Mod. Lang. Notes* XLIII 23; M Baring *Puppet Show of Memory* (1987) 142; W Lewis in C Fox *Journey Into Barbary* (1983) 153; H Price *Perception* 150; *TLS* 21 Apr. 284/4; J Masefield *Coll. Poems* 255; D Lawrence *Last Poems* 17; A Worral *Eng. Idioms* iii; L Wittgenstein in A Ambrose ed. *Wittgenstein's Lectures 1932-1935* 15; *Pol. Sci. Q.* XLIII 576; A Lindbergh *Hour of Gold* (1973) 290; S Knock *Clear Lower Deck 170.*

1933 H Wells *Shape of Things to Come* 396; H Ellis *Psychol. Sex* 37; O Jesperson *Essentials Eng. Grammar* (1954) 32; *Boy's Mag.* Apr. 90; H Allen *Anthony Adverse* 752; A Barton *Text-bk. Heat* 355; F Gough in A Gough *Gleanings* 9; L Bloomfield *Language* 173; W Taylor *Critique of Sublimation in Males* 89; J Powys *Glastonbury Romance* (1975) 157; G Robey *Looking Back on Life* 306; E Kellet *Literary Quotation & Allusion* 44/5; *Baltimore Sun* 13 May 18/2; J Brewer 'Old-Time Negro Proverbs' *Pub. Texas Folklore Soc.* XI 102.

1934 E Pound 'Teacher's Mission' in T Eliot ed. *Literary Essays E Pound* (1968) 58; W Lewis in *Essays on Art Lit. & Soc. 1914-1956* (1989) 217; *Jrnl. Amer. Statistical Assoc.* XXIX 89; A Goldie & R Abercrombie *Weather* (rev. ed.) 74; B Lewin & G Zilboorg tr. O Fenichel *Outline Clin. Psycho-anal.* 443; G Madan *Livre Sans Nom: Twelve Reflections* no.12 (in *Oxford Dict. Quotations* (1992) 441); *Jrnl. Amer. Medical Association* 13 Jan. 119/2; J Thomson *Biol. for Everyman* 198; *Amer. Home* July 71/1 (Advert); S Hutchison *North to the Rime-Ringed Sun* 111/2; *Discovery* Aug. 227/1; M Bodkin *Archetypal Patterns in Poetry* 254; R Tolman *Relativity, Thermodynamics & Cosmol.* 24; J Thomson *Biol. for Everyman* 339

1935 J O'Neill *Land Under England* (1978) 207; L MacNeice 'The Glacier' in *Poems* 52; E Bowen *House in Paris* (1983) 167; H Davis *Honey In Horn* 12; A Pollock *Underworld Speaks* 94/2; H Read *Green Child* (New Directions ed.) 161; *TLS* 7 Feb. 78/3; C Burge *Complete Bk. Aviation* 263/1; G Blake *Shipbuilders* (1986) 421; A Sullivan *Great Divide* 44; G Barker *Documents of a Death* 101; T Wolfe *Time & River* (1971) 58; *Motion Picture* Nov. 18 (Advt); M Anderson 'Winterset' in *Critics' Choice* I 33

1936 P Young *Motivation of Behaviour* 247; M Mitchell *Gone with Wind* (1962) 213; *Internat. Surrealist Bull.* IV 6; S Spender in *New Statesman* 11 Apr. 566/1; L Hogben *Maths. for the Million* (1995) 243; *Stage* June 57/2; J Buchan *Island of Sheep* 100; D Thomas in P Ferris ed. *Coll. Letters* (1987) 218; G Greene *Pleasure Dome* (1972) 76; *N.Y. Woman* 23 Sept. 9/1; *Lancet* 10 Oct. 865/2; D Barnes *Nightwood* (1949) 31; L Grinsell *Ancient Burial Mounds England* 37; M Anand *Coolie* (1993) 72.

1937 Y Winters *Primitiveness & Decadence* 26; R Carnap *Logical Syntax Lang.* 236; *Amer. Home* Apr. 136/4; R Wilson *Birth Lang.* 69; *Discovery* Mar. 65/2; *Kansas City Times* 16 June 19; J Marquand *Late George Apley* (1940) 112; Z Hurston *Their Eyes Were Watching God* (1990) 164; C Williams *Descent in Hell* (1949) 29; G Greene *Pleasure Dome* (1972) 162; *Life* 13 Sept. 21/2 (advert); D Hart-Davis *Hitler's Games* (1986) 235; *Sunday Times* 12 Dec. 5/1; *Complete Lyrics of L Hart* (1976) 236/2

1938 S Beckett *Murphy* (1963) 5; *Amer. Home* Jan. 76/3; H Read *Poetry & Anarchism* 15; E Bowen *Death of Heart* (1948) 205; *Life* 4 Apr. 4/2; *Sun* (Baltimore) 9 Aug. 20/1; J Gloag *Documents Marked 'Secret'* 1; *Mind* XLVII 260; V Woolf 26 June *Letters* (1980) VI. 246; D Baker *Young Man With Horn* (1978) 64; B Burman *Blow for Landing* 111; *Mississippi, Guide to State* 26; *Life* 6 June 1/1 (advert); E Queen *Four of Hearts* 295

1939 *Mind* XLV 504; T Green *Practical Animal Biol.* 149; E White 'Second World War' in *One Man's Meat* (1982) 85; F O'Brien *At Swim-Two-Birds* 277; *Trans. Faraday Soc.* XXXV 126; H Miller *Tropic of Capricorn* (1961) 236; W Fortescue *There's Rosemary* 366; *St. Nicholas* Aug. 37/3; *Amer. Jrnl. Sociol.* XLIV 925; N Blake *Smiler with Knife* 60; J Morton *Bonfire of Weeds* 63; *Fortune* Nov. 20/1; J Hendry 'Soldier's First Entry' in S Schimanski ed. *Leaves in Storm* (1947) 40; *Ice Cream Trade Jrnl.* 19 Nov. (advert)

1940 H Moore *Shelter Sketchbk.* (1988) 45; F Grout J *Kemp's Handbk. Rocks* (ed.6) 226; E O'Neill *Iceman Cometh* (1967) 61; T Eliot *East Coker* 8; *Kenyon Rev.* 270; E Birney *Sel. Poems* (1966) 123; D Powell *Angels on Toast* (1989) 15; H Mallalieu in B Gardner *Terrible Rain: War Poets: 1939-45* (1977) 50; Announcement for *Superman*, U.S. radio show; N Coward *Australia Visited* 10; N Eastman *Expectant Motherhood* (1947) 31; H Wells *Babes in Darkling Wood* 124; W Auden 'As I Walked Out One Evening' in *Coll. Poems* (1991) 134; A Ayer *Foundations Empirical Knowledge* 192

1941 J Burnham *Managerial Revolution* 229; R Heppenstall diary 8 Jan. in S Schimanski ed. *Leaves in Storm* (1947) 109; *British Jrnl. Psychol.* Jan. 232; A Koestler *Scum of Earth* 152; M Farquharson et al. *Gloss. Broadcasting Terms* 8; A Clarke *Coll. Plays* (1963) 133; J Agee *Let Us Now Praise Famous Men* (1988) 188; J Smiley *Hash House Lingo* 44; C Roth *Hist. Jews in England* 102; K Patchen *Jrnl. Albion Moonlight* (1961) 16; P Larkin 23 June in A Thwaite ed. *Sel. Letters* (1992) 16; W Lewis *Vulgar Streak* (1973) 85; Unnamed newspaper quoted 4 Sept. in D Gascoyne *Coll. Journals 1936-42* (1991) 312; T Roethke 'Open House' in *Open House* 13

1942 E Pound broadcast from Rome 30 Mar.; T Eliot *Little Gidding* 9; B Malinowski *Sci. Theory Culture* (1944) 20; J Berryman 'A Point of Age' *Poems* 18; *Public Opinion Q.* VI

474/2; *Mind* LI 319; Z Hurston *Dust Tracks on Road* 244; *Baltimore Sun* 19 June 1/4; *Daily Mirror* (NY) 7 Aug. 5/4; R Collingwood *New Leviathan* 42; C Adams *Private Eye* 100; *Lloyd's List Law Reports* LXIII 13/2; P Kavanagh *Great Hunger* 3; *Common Sense* II 351

1943 S Menefee *Assignment* 117; V Nabokov 'Mademoiselle O' in *Speak, Memory* (1966) 104; W Stegner *Big Rock Candy Mountain* (1991) 196; M Flavin *Journey in Dark* 174; W Guthrie *Bound For Glory* (1983) 136; J Bowles *Two Serious Ladies* (1979) 107; *Popular Science* (reprinted ibid. Oct. 1993 134/2); V Sackville-West *Eagle & Dove* 43; *Architectural Rev.* XCIV 135; *Mind* LII 129; J Huxley *TVA Adventure in Planning* 70; *Lancet* 26 June 815/1; A Fraas *Aircraft Power Plants* 172; *Nat. Geographic* Dec. 774/1 (advt)

1944 C Stevenson *Ethics & Lang.* 319; *Psychic Times* Feb. 3/3; A Pulford *Unsolved Mysteries* 14; A Comfort *Power House* 120; S Bellow *Dangling Man* (1946) 83; L Mumford *Condition of Man* 8; *Dan Burley's Original Handbk. Harlem Jive* 133; G Stein in S Schimanski ed. *Leaves in Storm* (1947) 236; M Myers *Yardbird Myers* 47; C Webb *Religious Experience* (1945) 29; Palinurus *Unquiet Grave* (1945) 63; W Beveridge *Full Employment in Free Soc.* 110; M Cohen *Preface to Logic* 82; F Hayek *Road to Serfdom* 115

1945 *Philos. Rev.* LIV 148; *Nature* in W Gratzer ed. *Bedside Nature* (1996) 240/2; V Bush 'As We May Think' *Atlantic Monthly* July; *Electronic Industries* Sept. 92; W Auden *For Time Being* 64; R Jarrell 'Death of the Ball Turret Gunner' in *Sel. Poems* (1990) 95; *William & Mary Q.* II 351; S Baker *Australian Lang.* 144; E Sitwell 'A Song of the Cold' in *Song of the Cold* 36; C Balleisen *Principles Firearms* 107; K Popper *Open Soc. & its Enemies* (1966) 1; P Larkin 31 Oct. *Sel. Letters* (1992) 110; *Jrnl. Philos.* XLII 433; R Collingwood *Idea of Nature* 175

1946 R Wilbur *Beautiful Changes* 3; E Bishop 'The Map' *North & South*; P Symonds *Dynamics Human Adjustment* 126; D Peattie *Road of Naturalist* 24; M Mezzrow *Really the Blues* 60; A Christie *Hollow* xvi; *Proc. British Acad.* XXXII 87; A Koestler *Thieves in Night* 173; *Liberty* 25 May 21/1; J Eckert in *Moore School Lectures* (1985) 245; A Nelson *Principles Agricultural Botany* 500; *Nature* 10 Aug. 185/1; C Ozick in *Metaphor & Memory* (1989) 118; R Collingwood *Idea of Hist.* 217

1947 G Cole *Intelligent Man's Guide to Post-War World* 515; J Rich *Materials & Methods Sculpture* 257; *Southern Folklore Q.* XI 263-7; *Science News* 4 38; H Nemerov 'Image & Law' in *Coll. Poems* (1977) 14; J Lowell *Dear Sir* 14; T Williams *Streetcar Named Desire* (1956) 144; A Imms *Outline Entomol.* (ed.3) 73; *Chicago Tribune* 21 June 2/5; *Baltimore Sun* 15 Sept. 3/1; *Penguin New Biol.* 3 88; E Partridge *Usage & Abusage* 363; *Nucleonics* Dec. 38/1; D Powell *Films Since 1939* 24

1948 L Whitby *Nurse's Handbk. Hygeine* (ed. 8) 89; *New Biol.* V 33; A Kinsey et al. *Sexual Behaviour in Human Male* 68/1; *Baltimore Sun* Mar. 12 4/3; *Annual Register for 1947* 387; *Life* 26 Apr. 43/1; J Morton *Molluscs* 97; S Bellow in *It All Adds Up* (1993) 189; S Perelman *Westward Ha!* 119; A Toynbee *Study of Hist.* (4th ed) 32; T Heggen *Mister Roberts* 33; *Yale French Stud.* no. 2 98; *Mind* LVII 4; *Life* 6 Sept. (inside front cover)

1949 G Ryle *Concept of Mind* 91; *Chicago Daily News* 4 May 14/7; T Birch *Maps — Topographical & Statistical* (1969) 21; M Mead *Male & Female* 262; *L.A. Times* 16 May 13/1; G Birmingham *Laura's Bishop* 141; W Burroughs 24 June in *Letters 1945-1959* (1994) 51; A Koestler *Insight & Outlook* 337; H Bailey *Demonstrations Phys. Signs in Clin. Surgery* (ed.11) 68; W Albright *Archaeol. Palestine* 185; G Orwell *1984* (Appendix) 302; E Pound *Pisan Cantos* lxxiv 30; V Nabokov in *Speak, Memory* (1966) 226; H Nicholson 25 July in *Diaries & Letters 1945-62* (1968) 173

1950 *Jrnl. Aviation Med.* XXI 396/2; E D M *St Philomena Wonder-worker* 17; H Leverenz *Introd. Luminescence Solids* 369; *Caribbean* Q. II 28; V Sackville-West 6 Feb. in *Diaries & Letters 1945-62* (1968) 185; W Tarn *Treasure Isle of Mist* 145; *Internat. Jrnl. Sexol.* III 148/1; *Science News* XV 84-85; *Baltimore Sun* 28 Sept. 9/4; *Chambers's Jrnl.* 254/2; J Cheever in H Brickell ed. *O.Henry Prize Stories* 1951 (1951); A Lee *Soviet Air Force* 155; S Perelman *Swiss Family Perelman* (1987) 121; W Stevens 'An Ordinary Evening in New Haven' 28 *Auroras of Autumn* 165

1951 J Custance *Wisdom Madness & Folly* 64; *TLS* 19 Jan. 12/1; D Jones 'Introduction' *Anathemata* (1979) 9; M Cowley *Exile's Return* 229; T Roethke *Straw for Fire* (1972) 207; M Sadleir preface *XIX Fiction: A Bibliog.; Baltimore Sun* 30 Mar. 32/4; H Arendt *Burden of Our Time* 291; V Nabokov in *Speak, Memory* (1966) 265; J Agee *Morning Watch* (1975) 57; R Chandler 19 Apr. in F MacShane ed. *Sel. Letters* (1981) 271; E Bowen *Shelbourne* 172; E Bergler 'Premature Ejaculation' in *Sel. Papers* (1969) 653; *Baltimore Sun* 26 Dec. 4/4

1952 G Dury *Map Interpretation* 74; F Moorhouse *Maps & Diagrams* (1969) 373; S Perelman in *Road to Miltown* (1957) 254; C Blacker *Eugenics Galton & After* 68; M McCarthy *Groves of Academe* (1953) 84; J Steinbeck *East of Eden* (1958) 114; A Norton *Daybreak — 2250 A.D.* 18; E Hobsbaum in J Philip et al. *Best of Granta* (1967) II 114; B Ulanov *Hist. Jazz in America* 157; *Statements by Two Amer. Air Force Officers Admitting Participation in Germ Warfare in Korea* 3; E Sykes *Everyman's Dict. Non-classical Mythol.* 142; J Thompson *Killer Inside Me* (1991) 180; *Good Housekeeping* Dec. 133/1; *Penguin New Biol.* XIII 103

1953 L Hartley *Go-Between* (1958) 77; M Powys *Lace & Lace-Making* 31; J Cary *Except the Lord* 79; S Brown in A Dundes *Mother Wit* (1973) 41/2; J Wain *Hurry on Down* (1960) 181; *Architectural Rev.* CXIII 122; *Mind* LXII 457; *Life* 8 June 64 (advt); E Hutton *Assisi & Umbria Revisited* 150; A Flew *New Approach to Psychical Research* 91; E Wilkin & E Kaiser tr. E Musil *Man Without Qualities* (1980) 152; L Wittgenstein *Philos. Investigations* 11; A Pearse *Histochemistry* 454; J Hawkes *A Land* 27

1954 D Thomas *Under Milk Wood* 8; P Frankau *Wreath for Enemy* (1988) 26; I Murdoch *Under Net* (1960) 16; *Philos. Rev.* LXIII 391; *Mod. Lang. Notes* LXV 283; T Eliot *Confidential Clerk* 58; E Alport in L Sweet *Peoples & Cultures Middle East* II (1970) 235; E Muir *Autobiog.* (1993) 111; *Amer. Jrnl. Roentgenol. Radiation Therapy & Nuclear Medicine* LXXII 591/1; J Hadfield *Dreams & Nightmares* 189; A Huxley *Doors of Perception* (1960) 41; W March *Bad Seed* (1978) 92; A Koestler *Invisible Writing* 400; J Tolkien *Fellowship of Ring* 141

1955 R Thomas *Song at Year's Turning* 52; A Huxley 10 Jan. *Letters* (1969) 720; H Marcuse *Eros & Civilization* 39; F Ashbrook *Butchering, Processing & Preservation Meat* v; G Gorer *Exploring Eng. Character* 192; B Spock *Baby & Child Care* (1969) 597; words on billboard in W Klein photograph, exhibited Edinburgh 1998; M Stewart *Madam, Will You Talk?* (1961) 107; *Science News Letter* 27 Oct. 130; R Lindner *50-Minute Hour* (1986) 95; *Baltimore Sun* Nov. 21 1/6; A Ginsberg *Coll. Poems* (1988) 126; *Pacific Reporter* CCLXXXVIII 560; F Caprio *Variations in Sexual Behaviour* 39

1956 *Amer. Speech* 287; W Bird *Off-Trail in Nova-Scotia* 87; N Algren *Walk on Wild Side* (1992) 174; E Mascall *Christian Theol. & Natural Science* 134; *Brit. Bk. of Year* 493/1; J Kent in B Beard ed. *Smithsonian Coll. Newspaper Comics* (1977) 316; L McIntosh *Oxford Folly* 153; H Nicolson 9th Feb. in *Diaries & Letters* (1968) 298; L Durrell *Justine* ii; *Life* 2 Apr. 21/2 (advt); R Bourne *Hist. Literary Radical* 66; A Wilson *Anglo-Saxon Attitiudes* 365;

Time (Canad. Edition) 10 Dec. 16/3; Kim Il Sung *Report Central Committee Worker's Party Korea to Third Congress* 130

1957 *Science* CXXVI 305/3; N Chomsky *Syntactic Structures* 18; B Evans & C Evans *Dict. Contemp. Amer. Usage* 152/1; C Vereker *Development Political Theory* 147; R Hoggart *Uses Literacy* 34; School of D McGill postcard in T Phillips ed. *Postcard Century* (2000) 264; F Kohner *Gidget* 44; J Adams *Outline Fractures* 157; *Observer* 3 Nov. 14/6; H Miller *Tropic of Capricorn* (1966) 135; G Hutchinson *Treatises on Limnol.* 257; R Carew Hunt *Guide Communist Jargon* 42; *Penguin New Biol.* XXII 60; T Jeffcoate *Principles Gynaecol.* 559

1958 *New Statesman* 22 Feb. 223/2; K Rexroth 'Jazz Poetry' in B Morrow *World Outside Window* (1987) 71; W Stark *Sociol. Knowledge* 137; J Barth *End of Road* 110; R Brown *Words & Things* 82; G Leff *Medieval Thought* 70; *Architectural Rev.* CXXIII 310; W Williams *Paterson* 137; J Wain *Contenders* (1962) 132; *Life* 19 May 57/1; *Times* 27 June 6/3; P Gibbs *Curtains of Yesteryear* 120; *Spectator* 19 Sept. 379/1; G Greene *Our Man in Havana* 101; *Listener* 11 Dec. 983/2

1959 S Watson *Double Hook* 48; A Nin *Children of Albatross* 56; W Penfield & L Roberts *Speech & Brain Mechanisms* 47; *IBM Jrnl.* III 211/1; J Cheever *Journals* (1991) 110; A Koestler *Sleepwalkers* (1968) 329; *Listener* 9 Apr. 647/2; H Hobson *Mission House Murder* 13; R Bradbury *Day it Rained Forever* (1963) 182; S Watson *Double Hook* 29; P Larkin 15 Sept. in A Thwaite ed. *Sel. Letters* (1992) 307; *Which?* Nov. 152/1; *Listener* 29 Oct. 720/3; J Berryman *77 Dream Songs* 84

1960 *Nature* 14 May 559/1; D Braungart & R Buddeke *Introd. Animal Biol.* (ed 5) 174; C Day Lewis *Buried Day* 15; *Colston Research Soc. Symposium* XII 90; *Current Anthropol.* I 295; R Williams *Border Country* (1978) 160; F Mann & B Saunders *Practical Organic Chemistry* (ed 4) 62; K Patchen *Because It Is* 27; S Plath *Colossus* 63; N Moore *Proud Walk* 310; J Cheever *Journals* (1991) 138; P Tappan *Crime, Justice & Correction* 62; C Geertz *Religion Java* 30; H Nemerov in *Coll. Poems* (1977) 221

1961 *New Scientist* 23 Feb. 472/1; J Updike *Rabbit, Run* (1974) 45; *Vogue* 15 April 82; W Brandon *Indians* (1987) 25; I Clarke *Tale of Future* 10; H Thompson 14 Aug. *Letters* (1998); *Time* 29 Dec. 26; *Aeroplane & Astronautics* 101 92/2; *Muscle Power* Nov. 25/2; P Wodehouse *Ice in Bedroom* 11; G Durrell *Whispering Land* (1965) 152; K Reisz *Technique Film Editing* (ed 9) 269; H D *Helen in Egypt* (1985) 183; E Bruton *Dict. Clocks & Watches* 180

1962 *Mod. Lang. Notes* LXXVII 71; S Wynter *Hills Hebron* 70; R Bly 'After Drinking All Night With a Friend' in *Silence in Snowy Fields*; A Sexton 'All My Pretty Ones' in *Sel. Poems* (1964) 93; *Flight Internat.* LXXXI 283/1; *Daily Tel.* 22 May 24/6; *Time* 25 May 70/3; *Transition* no. 5 33; W McEwen in H Davson *Eye* III 272; M McLuhan *Gutenberg Galaxy* 63; W Nowottny *Lang. Poets Use* 131; *Lancet* 29 Dec. 1374/1; *Listener* 12 July 51/1; A Whitehead & B Russell *Principia Mathematica* 61.

1963 H Baade *Jurimetrics* 215; *Proc. San Diego Symposium on Biomed. Engineering* 199/1; R Carson *Silent Spring* (1965) 50; V Nabokov *Gift* 86; *Punch* 2 Jan. 6/2; *Listener* 7 Feb. 260/3; *Oxford Mail* 25 Feb. 3/6; *TLS* 26 Apr. 295/3; *B.S.I. News* Apr. 32; *Annual Register* 1962 403; R Carnap in P Schilpp *Philos. R Carnap* 961; D MacDonald *Against Amer. Grain* 58; D Matheson tr. F Schuon *Understanding Islam* (1976) 48; *Times* 10 May 22

1964 J Berryman 'Dream Song' in *77 Dream Songs* 82; E Baxter *Fine Madness* 207; H Thompson 28 Apr. *Letters* (1998); G Legman *Horn-bk.: A Study in Erotic Folklore* 29; G

Cohen *What's Wrong With Hospitals?* 113; S Bellow *Herzog* (1967) 138; J Meerloo *Hidden Communion* 110; F Bowers *Bibliog. & Textual Criticism* 151; M McLuhan *Understanding Media* 313; L Woolf *Beginning Again* 164; F Westwater *Electronic Computers* 143; *Lang.* XL 81; *Courier-Mail* (Brisbane) 1 Dec. (unpaginated); L Martin *Clin. Endocrinol.* (ed.4) 62.

1965 H Kahn *On Escalations* 172; J Carthy *Behaviour Arthropods* 6; B Freeman tr. A Vandel *Biospeleol.* 24; W Golding in *Hot Gates* (1970) 63; H Gold *Man Who Was Not With It* 275; L Ferlinghetti in *Wholly Communion* 24; P Wylie *They Both Were Naked* 138; S Plath 'Morning Song' in *Ariel; New Scientist* 19 Aug. 456/1; T Pynchon *Crying Lot 49* (1979) 84; *New Statesman* 8 Oct. 542/4; B Behan *Confessions Irish Rebel* (1967) 40; *Sunday Express* 10 Oct. 6/2; M Frayn *Tin Men* 81

1966 *Philos. Rev.* LXXV 315; *Punch* 2 Feb. 160/1; *Monumenta Nipponica* XXII 91; J Barth *Giles Goat-Boy* (1967) 215; *Time* 1 July 50; F Stillman *Poet's Manual & Rhyming Dict.* (1985) 314; *Bulletin Narcotics* XVIII 6/2; Graffito on IRT, Broadway Line, NY, in *Maledicta* 29; L Lane *ABZ of Scouse* 81-2; *New Statesman* 22 July 125/3; F Shaw et al *Lern Yerself Scouse* 45; T Corlett & D Osborne *Devel. Reading Frequency Scales* 5/1; *Economist* 8 Oct. 162/2-3; *Atlantic Monthly* Oct. 14

1967 E Liebow in T Kochman *Rappin' & Stylin' Out* (1972) 405; G Davis in W King *Black Short Story Anthol.* (1972) 341; *N.Y. Times* (Internat. ed.) 11-12 Feb. 1/5; E Bleiler tr. E Hoffman in E Rabkin ed. *Science Fiction: A Hist. Anthol.* (1983) 105; Taylor postcard caption in T Phillips ed. *Postcard Century* (2000) 304; *Transition* no.33 57; M Ayrton *Maze Maker* 130; *Brain* XC 260; G Steiner *Lang. & Silence* 233; *British Jrnl. Psychiatry* CXIII 1050/2; E Lea in R Masters *Sexual Self-Stimulation* 325; *Datamation* Feb. 29/2; *Oxford Computer Explained* 7; *Archives Neurol.* 17 100/2;

1968 M McLuhan 3 June in M Molinaro et al ed. *Letters* (1987) 352; *NY Times* 27 June 35/2; T Wolfe *Electric Kool-aid Acid Test* 60; P McKellar *Experience & Behaviour* 120; *Jrnl. Pediatrics* LXXIII 692/2; *British Jrnl. Psychiatry* CXIV 1482/1; V Nabokov *King, Queen, Knave* (1989) 29; N Mosley *Impossible Object* 130; D Braithwaite *Fairground Architecture* 168; *British Medical Bull.* XXIV 197/2; M Black *Labyrinth Lang.* 66; P Moran *Introd. Probability Theory* 134; *Oz* 14 Dec. 11; B Smith *Poetic Closure* 34.

1969 *Jrnl. Philos.* LXVI 15; V Nabokov *Ada* 359; *Proc. Royal Soc. (Math. & Phys. Sci.)* 338; *Product Engineering* 27 Jan. 15/3; *Sunday Times Colour Suppl.* 23 Feb.18; *Gloss. Terms Dentistry* (B.S.I.) 50; E Pinto *Treen* 147-148; *Tanzania Notes & Records* July 6; *Encycl. Science Suppl.* 329; *Gloss. Acoustical Terms* (B.S.I.) 13; M Sharpe *Living in Space* 60; *Nature* 24 May 763/1; R Lowell *Notebk.* (1970) 37; A Smith *Discovering Folklore in Industry* 40.

1970 *Redemption Tidings* 23 Apr. 8/1; J McConnell *Eton Repointed* 42; G Newman *Sir, You Bastard* 213; J Dickey *Deliverance* 25; R Hoppe et al. *Early Experiences & Process Socialisation* 82; G Germani in I Horowitz *Masses in Latin America* 303; C Storr *Unnatural Fathers* 88; *Computers & Humanities* V 4; B Brewster tr. L Althusser & E Balibar *Reading Capital* (1975) 292; D Jacobson *Rape of Tamar* (1980) 19; R Abrahams *Positively Black* 26; C Major *Dict. Afro-Amer. Slang* 97; C Irving *Fake!* 234; L Jeffers 'My Blackness is the Beauty of This Land' in S Henderson *Understanding New Black Poetry* (1973) 198

1971 A Gouldner *Coming Crisis Western Sociol.* 47-8 (cited in K Hudson *Jargon of Professions* (1978) 88); *Sunday Truth* (Brisbane) 21 Feb. 40/1; W Hanley *Blue Dreams* 224; *Jrnl. Philos.* LXVIII 208; D Parfit 'Personal Identity' in T Honderich & M Burnyeat *Philos. as it Is* (1979) 202; *British Medical Bull.* XXVII 56/1; *Power Farming* Mar. 71/1;

Family Planning Perspectives III 62; D Morris *Intimate Behaviour* 161; *Frendz* 21 May 11/1; *Sci. Amer.* Sept. 228/3; *World Archaeol.* III 136; B Cole *Bk. Rook* 178; D Sciama *Mod. Cosmol.* 133

1972 M Shadbolt *Strangers & Journeys* 3; *Gloss. Aeronautical & Astronautical Terms* (B.S.I.) XV s.v. 'rain'; *McGraw-Hill Yearbk. Science & Technol.*, 1971 376/2; J Berger G 155; *Times* 6 Apr. 7; W Samarin *Tongues of Men & Angels* 203; *Accountant* 6 Apr. 453/1; *Daily* Tel. 1 June 13/2; *Village Voice* 1 June 67/3; J Campbell *Myths to Live By* (1988) 84; *Computers & Humanities* VII 6; C Buchanan *Maiden* 2; *Awake!* 8 Nov. 3/1; *Sci. Amer.* Dec. 71/1

1973 E Jong *Fear of Flying* (1974) 55; *Times* 1 Feb. 23/6; *Physics Bull.* Feb. 76/2; C Blaise 'Bridge' in *North Amer. Education* (1984) 134; E. Heron-Allen *Violin-Making* 135; D Kyle *Raft of Swords* 122; *Art Internat.* Mar. 75/2; M Fisher 'Wind-Chill Factor' in *As They Were* (1982) 220; H Gruppe *Truxton Cipher* 134; H Nieburg *Culture Storm* 132; *Philadelphia Enquirer* (Sunday Supp.) 7 Oct. 32 (advt.); T Pynchon *Gravity's Rainbow* (1975) 133; *Daily Colonist* (Victoria, B.C.) 28 July 24/4; *Nat. Observer* (U.S.) 3 Nov. 1.

1974 M Taylor tr. C Metz *Film Lang.* 76; M Gerald *Pharmacol.* 201; *Gloss. Terms Plastics Industry* (B.S.I.) II 5; A Murakami *Romanized Japanese* (1979) 24; V Mountcastle *Med. Physiol.* (ed.13) 1316/2; *Evening Herald* (Rock Hill, S Carolina) 18 Apr. 2/3; *Bookseller* 10 Aug. 999/2 (advt); 'Script & Film' in *Bks. in Canada* 42; *Nature* 4 Oct. 414/1; M Ayrton *Midas Consequence* (1978) 40; E Bowen *Henry & Other Heroes* 59; R Crossman *Diaries* (1976) II 593; M Brown *Econ. Imperialism* 60; *Times* 3 Dec. 14/5

1975 R Howard tr. E Cioran *Short Hist. Decay* 26; *Aviation Week & Space Technol.* 6 Jan. 17; J Russ *Female Man* 7; T Berger *Sneaky People* 305; D & E Riesman *Conversations in Japan* 282; H Acton *Nancy Mitford* 57; G Legman *No Laughing Matter* 87; T Struhsaker *Red Colobus Monkey* plate 8; J Stewart *Gaudy* 16; *New Yorker* 19 May 40/3; J Tweedie in *Manchester Guardian* Nov. 10; F Exley *Pages from Cold Island* (1988) 35; W Safire *Before Fall* 331; *Mind* LXXXIV 168

1976 *Nat. Observer* (U.S.) 10 Jan. 2/5; *Aviation Week & Space Technol.* 19 Jan. 36; *New Yorker* 8 Mar. 125/1; *Milton Keynes Express* 11 June 2/5; *Billings* (Montana) *Gaz.* 28 June 1/2; *Toronto Star* 21 Aug. B1/2; *Eastern Evening News* (Norwich) 27 Aug. 1/1; *Daily* Tel. 23 Sept. 11/1; *Southern Evening Echo* (Southampton) 12 Nov. 11/1; *Globe & Mail* (Toronto) 13 Nov. 16/5; *Leicester Chron.* 26 Nov. 17/3; *Star* (Sheffield) 29 Nov. 8/4; *Ilkeston Advertiser* 10 Dec. 8/7

1977 *Gay News* 24 Mar. 23/3; *Grimsby Evening* Tel. 27 May 18/7-8; U Eco 'Semiotics of Theatrical Performance' in D Walder ed. *Lit. in Mod. World* (1990) 117; *Annual Internat. Medicine* LXXXVI 368/1; J Douglas *Existential Sociol.* 24; H Boas 'Transpositional & Semantic Adjectives' in D Kastovsky *Perspektiven der Wortbildungs* 23; A Hallam *Planet Earth* 17/3; W Merwin *Compass Flower* 35; *Time* 25 Apr. 50/1; *Time Out* 17-23 June 16/1; D Morris *Manwatching* 185; J Weeks *Coming Out* 214; *Annual Internat. Medicine* LXXXVI 590/2; *Transatlantic Rev.* LX 109

1978 S Chatman 'Story & Narrative' in D Walder ed. *Lit. in Mod. World* (1991) 108; *Eng. Lit. Hist.* XVL162; I & I Kesarcodi tr. V Lossky *Orthodox Theol.* (1989) 99; *Beano* 8 Apr. 4; R Reddy in A Hanson & E Riseman *Computer Vision Systems* 89/1; *Detroit Free Press* 14 Apr. 12/2; J Cheever *Stories* (1980) 715; *Lang.* LIV 482; P Pettit in C Hookway & P Pettit *Action & Interpretation* 61; *Daedalus* Fall 154; P Howard *Weasel Words* 31; *Jrnl. Technical Writing & Communication* VIII 313; N Marsh *Grave Mistake* 72; *Globe & Mail* (Toronto) 11 Nov. 8/3

1979 *Philos. Q.* XXIX 222; *Time* 8 Jan. 62/3; D Kessler in C Fora *Making Musical Instruments* 19; A Storr *Art Psychotherapy* 43; *Maledicta* III 74; A Paul in C Fora *Making Musical Instruments* 69; *Contemp. Sociol.* VIII 495/1; L Blue *Backdoor to Heaven* (1985) 77; *Tel.* (Brisbane) 15 June 6/1; C Lasch *Culture Narcissism* 65; F Kermode *Genesis Soc.* 72; *Amer. Speech* LIV 75; *Jrnl. Near Eastern Stud.* XXXVIII 258; N Gordimer *Burger's Daughter* 182

1980 M Robinson *Housekeeping* (1991) 90; W Percy *Second Coming* 275; D Lodge *How Far Can You Go?* (1981) 15; W Berry 'Solving for Pattern' in *Gift of Good Land* (1981) 138; R Bushby in K Thear & A Fraser *Complete Bk. Raising Livestock & Poultry* (1988) 148/1; G Priestland *At Large* (1983) 27; *Bulletin* (Australia) 26 Feb. 5; *Search* XI 69/1; *Nous* XIV 451; *Observer* (Rev. section) 2 Mar. 40/5-6; *N.Y. Times* 10 Aug. VII 26/2; R Crumb 'My Trouble With Women' in *My Troubles With Women* 1990 (unpaginated); *Maledicta* IV 194; G Kinnell *Mortal Acts, Mortal Words* 54

1981 L Lapham 'Theater of News' in *Imperial Masquerade* (1990) 12; *Nat. Times* (Australia) 25-31 Jan. 24/2; P Kerr in T Bennett et al. *Popular T.V. & Film* 75; C Potok *Bk. of Lights* 9; D Rutherford *Porcupine Basin* 30; T Boyle *Water Music* (1983) 4; E Sedgwick 'Jane Austen & the Masturbating Girl' in *Tendencies* (1993) 117; *Mining Annual Rev.* June 491; *Jrnl. Steroid Biochemistry* XXI 14; S Flower et al. *Debrett's Etiquette & Mod. Manners* 279; *Philos. Q.* XXXI 158; B Dixon 'Shape Shapes Shape' in O Davies ed. *Omni Bk. Paranormal & Mind* 139; J Fonda *Workout Bk.* 155; C Bly *Letters from Country* 72

1982 R Selzer *Confessions of a Knife* 10; M Duke *Flashpoint* 46; A Road Dr *Who: Making of TV Series* 37/2; *Times* 12 Feb. 17/1; J Culler *On Deconstruction* (1983) 209; *NY Times* 14 Feb. section 7, 1/1; W Least Heat-Moon *Blue Highways* (1991) 198; K Pollitt *Antarctic Traveller* 54; *Daily Tel.* 3 May 16/7; *Giant Bk. Electron. Projects* 68; *Sci. Amer.* July 99/3; *TLS* 23 July 801/1; W Hatcher *Logical Foundations Maths.* 203; *Eng. Lit. Hist.* IL 200.

1983 *Wall Street Jrnl.* 5 Jan. 4/5; *Man* XVIII 1; *Amer. Midland Naturalist* 427; *Amer. Jrnl. Forensic Med. Pathol.* IV 341/2; W Rowe *Clapp's Rock* 327; *NY Times* 16 Mar. 132/1; *Sci. Amer.* Apr. 95; R Scruton *Aesthetic Imagination* 154; *Oxford Bk. Death* xi; J Macy *Despair & Personal Power* xiv; P de Man *Rhetoric Romanticism* (1984) 287; T Eagleton in D Walder ed. *Lit. in Mod. World* (1990) 24; *NY Times* 29 Aug. B3/1; *Amer. Speech* LVIII 47

1984 A Lee *Sarah Phillips* (1985) 99; C Ozick *Cannibal Galaxy* 87; E De Garmo et al *Materials & Processes in Manufacture* (ed. 6) 977; P Winston *Artificial Intelligence* 278; J Lowe & M Walker *Reconstructing Quaternary Environments* 319; M Taussig *Processes in Pathol. & Microbiol.* (ed 2) 292; J Gash *Gondola Scam* (1985) 109; J Lamb et al. *Essential Physiol.* (ed.2) 291; R Saner *Essay on Air* 47; *Anthroposophical Rev.* VI 10; *NY Times Bk. Rev.* 1 Apr. 32/2; *Women's Wear Daily* 11 May 14; *Washington Post* 3 July 1; E Goodland tr. M de Andrade *Macunaima* 30

1985 R Howard tr. R Barthes *Responsibility of Forms* 162; J Roberts *Triumph of West* 214; C Leeson et el. *Textbk. Histol.* (ed. 5) 355/1; P Curran *Principles Remote Sensing* 24; L Waterland *Read With Me* 9; G Ehrlich *Solace of Open Spaces* 63; *Adweek* Mar. 6; J Merrill *Late Settings* 47; *Observer* 10 Mar. 47/6; *Sunday Times* 31 Mar. 39/4; *Verbatim* Summer 6/1; *Vogue* July 44 (advt); *Sci. Amer.* Aug. 14/1; J Isbister *Freud* 97

1986 *Evening Tel.* (Grimsby) 3 Apr. 10 (advt); *Courier Mail* (Brisbane) 7 June 53/1; A Romer & T Parsons *Vertebrate Body* (ed. 6) 594; *MacDonald Encycl. Fossils* 40; W Weaver tr. U Eco *Travels in Hyperreality* 5; *San Diego Union Tribune* 2 July AI; *New England Jrnl. Medicine* 22 May (unpaginated advt); G Chesbro *Veil* (1987) 46; D Madden *Hidden*

Symptoms (1988) 63; T Maddox 'Snake Eyes' in B Sterling *Mirrorshades* 21; *Toronto Star* 5 July M4; *NY Times* Aug. 10 (section 7) 3/1; R Goldenson & K Anderson *Sex A-Z* 173/1

1987 B Duffy *World as I Found It* (1990) 85; A Colman *Facts, Fallacies & Frauds in Psychol.* 174; *Science* CCXXXV161; *TLS* 10 Apr. 395/2; R Brindle *New Music* (ed. 2) 158; R Wilbur 'To the Etruscan Poets' in *The Mind-Reader* 241; J Franklin *Molecules of Mind* (1988) 109; V Stern *Bricks of Shame* (1989) 235; M Laverack & J Dando *Lecture Notes Invertebrate Zool.* (ed 3) 42; E Burr *Companion Bird Medicine* 161/1; J Waters *Crackpot* (1988) 18; G Larson *Far Side Observer* 70/1; *Yale French Stud.* LXXIII 34; J Holm 'Introd.' to T Salter *Mirrhor of Modestie* 23.

1988 M Bradbury *Unsent Letters* (1988) 173; N Postman *Conscientious Objections* 139; M McLuhan 'Role of New Media in Social Change' in G Lynch & D Rampton *Canad. Essay* (1991) 119; A Danto 'Diebenkorn' in *Encounters & Reflections* (1991) 194; *Courier-Mail* (Brisbane) 12 Mar. (Weekend Suppl.) 3/6; *Literary Rev.* Aug. 45/1; M Brodsky *X in Paris* 179; R Ellman 'Ductile Universe of Henri Michaux' in *a long the riverrun* (1988) 192; R Hall *Kisses of Enemy* (1990) 309; R Shilts *Band Played On* 153; N Bissoondath *Casual Brutality* 18; D Glover 'Why I Decide to Kill Myself' in M Atwood ed. *Best Amer. Short Stories* 1988 (1989); *Paragraph* XI 208; B Cooper *A Isbister* 61

1989 A Danto 'Warhol' in *Encounters & Reflections* (1991) 288; R Alter *Pleasures of Reading* 114; *British Jrnl. Philos. Science* XL 515; *Spy* (N.Y.) Mar. 94/1; *TLS* 9 June 634/1; *Third Text* Summer 36; *Sci. Amer.* July 61/2; A Jeffreys in J Durant *Human Origins* 134; *Brain* CXII 874; *Oxford Handbk. Clin. Specialties* (ed. 2) 232; *Amer. Q.* 274; A Dillard *Writing Life* 20; S Bradfield *Hist. of Luminous Motion* (1990) 85; R Banks *Affliction* 48

1990 A Kernan *Death of Lit.* 206; *Poetry Rev.* Spring 52/1; *Brain* CXIII 402; R Rhodes *Hole in World* 242; *Boston Phoenix* 27 Apr.-3 May 3/5; G Snyder *Practice of Wild* 66; *Jrnl. Logic & Computation* I 2; *Sci. Amer.* 94/3; *New Scientist* 28 July 32/3; *Practical Computing* Sept. 35/3; *ICL Technical Jrnl.* VII 386; *Star-Ledger* (Newark) 28 Oct. 19/1; *Raritan* IX 2; *Harvard Jrnl. Asiatic Stud.* L 547

1991 *Atlantic* Jan. 82/2; R Howard tr. E Cioran *Anathemas & Admirations* 140; *Mind* C 130; *Gander Mountain Archery Catalogue* 38/3; J Makower et al. *Green Consumer Supermarket Guide* 88; *British Med. Jrnl.* 9 Mar. 598/3; *Science News* 9 Mar. 158/3; *New Art Examiner* Apr. 41/2; *Whole Earth Rev.* Summer 55/3; *Lancet* 3 Aug. vi; F Buechner *Telling Secrets* 32; *Time* 25 Nov. 98/2; *Newsweek* 9 Dec. 55; *H James Rev.* I 86

1992 *Newsweek* 6 Jan. 4/1; *Callaloo* XV 167; *Acta Victoriana* Feb. 17/2; *Leisure Opportunities* 17 Feb. 5/1; *Economist* 14 Mar. 90/1; *Independent* 11 May 15/8; *City Limits* 2-9 July 12/2; A Gore *Earth in Balance* 252; *Canad. Geographic* July/Aug. 48/2; *Globe & Mail* (Toronto) 6 Aug. (Fashion supplement) 1/2; *Canad. Interiors* Oct. 50; *New Scientist* 3 Oct. 18/2; *Industry Week* 7 Dec. 56 (advt); *Mind* CI 185

1993 *Making of Jurassic Park* 152 (caption); *Equinox* Mar. 78/1; A Thomson *Virtual Girl* 146; *Proc. Biol. Sci.* (Royal Soc.) CCLII 7; *Time Out* 31 Mar.-7 Apr. 150/4; C Tilley *Interpretive Archaeol.* 186; *Sci. Amer.* Apr. 15/1; R Rucke et al. *Mondo 2000* 128/1; *Guardian* 28 July 8/1; M Novak 'Liquid Architectures in Cyberspace' in M Benedikt ed. *Cyberspace* (1993) 244; *New Scientist* 14 Aug. 27/1; *Radio Times* 18 Sept. 88/1; *Ideal Home* Sept. 35/1; *Family Therapy Networker* Sept.-Oct. 2/2

1994 *Post* (Denver) 2 Jan. 19/1; *Post* (Denver) 9 Jan. 6/2; *Daily Tel.* 10 Jan. 16/1; *NY Times* 11 Jan. 13/4; J Barth *Once Upon Time* 121; *Daily Tel.* 28 Feb. (advt); *Sci. Amer.* Mar.

54/2; *Esquire* Mar. 78/1; J Lattis *Between Copernicus & Galileo* 73; *Prairie Fire* Summer 220; *Magnet* July 32/1; *Inside Soap* Aug. 19/3; B Hambly *Crossroad* 44; R Preston *Hot Zone* 84

1995 *Proc. IEEE Internat. Conference on Neural Networks* IV 2014; *Amer. Scientist* Jan.-Feb. 26/2; *Chain Store Age Executive* (advt.) Aug. (unpaginated); *Boston Bk. Rev.* Apr. 21/1; G Harris in C Hollin *Contemp. Psychol.* II 75; *Sky & Telescope* May 98/1; *New Scientist* 13 May 8/2; *New Yorker* 27 Mar. 59/1; *etc Montréal* 15 May — 15 Aug. 33/1; *Guardian* 15 June (OnLine Suppl.) 2/4; *Financial Rev.* (Sydney) 29 June 4/2; *Loaded* July 16/4; *Time* 24 July (inside front cover); *i-D* Aug. 22/1

1996 C Ess ed. *Philos. Perspectives in Computer Mediated Communication* 1; E Gregory *Quotation & Mod. Amer. Poetry* 2; C Bendon *Crossover* 3; *Film Q.* 22 Mar. 27; *Nat. Enquirer* 9 Apr. 32; N Baker 'Lumber' in *Size of Thoughts* 229; J Oates *We Were Mulvaneys* 33; *Nature* 2 May 24/1; *Observer* 5 May (reviews) 5/5; *US News & World Report* 29 July 64/1; *WEBTechniques* Aug. 10/1; *London Rev. Bks.* 5 Sept. 19/1; *Irish Times* 18 Sept. 14; *Jrnl. Material Culture* I 338

1997 D Skafte *When Oracles Speak* ix; *Rev. Eng. Stud.* XLVIII 2/3; R Jarvis *Romantic Writing & Pedestrian Travel* 195; *Hollywood Reporter* Mar. 21; D Delillo *Underworld* 514; *N.Y. Times* 7 Sept. section ii. 74/1; *Time Out* 10 Sept. 14/4; *Liverpool Echo* 18 Sept. 3/1; R Youngson *Medical Curiosities* 295; D Wiger *Clin. Documentation Sourcebk.* xi; *Daily Tel.* 24 Sept. 23/5; *Esquire* Nov. 65/2; *New Scientist* 22 Nov. 52/1; *Church Times* 28 Nov. 18/2

1998 *Lang. & Speech* XLI 46; *Lang. in Soc.* XXVII 496; *Natural Lang. & Linguistic Theory* XVI 283; *Poetry NZ* XVII 77; *Int. Rev. Appl. Linguistics* XXXVI 104; A Sanchez-Macorro ed. *Linguistic Choice across Genres* 34; E Higgs ed. *Hist. & Electronic Artefacts* 162; *Water & Waste Treatment* June 49/4; *New Scientist* 18 July 37/3; *Guardian* 1 Aug. 3/2; *Lang.* LXXIV 313; *Neophilologus* LXXXII 550; *Tel.* 26 Aug. 5/4; *MLQ* LIX 406

1999 J Berry *Culture & Semiotics of Meaning* 58; *Hist. Today* Jan. 18/2; *London Rev. Bks.* 21 Jan. 24/2; *New Scientist* 23 Jan. 35/3; *Guardian* (review) 30 Jan. 5/4; *Record* (Bergen County, NJ) 14 Feb. A1; *Courier-Mail* (Brisbane) 5 Apr. 12/3; *Jerusalem Post* 22 Aug. 11; *N.Y. Times* 12 Sept. IV. 2/1; *Independent* 20 Sept. 15/6; *Bristol Evening Post* 16 Nov.; *Daily Tel.* 18 Nov. 1/6; *Radio Times* 18 Dec. 188/3; P Childs *Twentieth Century in Poetry* 204.

Also published by Leviathan

Roger Finch
Fox in the Morning
ISBN 1-903563-05-4 (cased)
1-903563-06-2 (paperback)

Stephanos Papadopoulos
Lost Days
ISBN 1-903563-02-X (cased)
1-903563-07-0 (paperback)

Jackie Wills
Party
ISBN 1-903563-03-8 (cased)
1-903563-04-6 (paperback)

Kit Wright
Hoping It Might Be So
ISBN 1-903563-00-3 (cased)
1-903563-01-1 (paperback)